Feminist Utopianism & Education

Educating for the Good Society

By

Christine Forde
Faculty of Education
University of Glasgow
UK

SENSE PUBLISHERS
ROTTERDAM / TAIPEI

A C.I.P. record for this book is available from the Library of Congress.

ISBN 978-90-8790-057-1 (paperback)
ISBN 978-90-8790-058-8 (hardback)

Published by: Sense Publishers,
P.O. Box 21858, 3001 AW Rotterdam, The Netherlands
http://www.sensepublishers.com

Printed on acid-free paper

FEMINIST UTOPIANISM & EDUCATION

EDUCATIONAL FUTURES
RETHINKING THEORY AND PRACTICE
Volume 9

Scope
This series maps the emergent field of educational futures. It will commission books on the futures of education in relation to the question of globalisation and knowledge economy. It seeks authors who can demonstrate their understanding of discourses of the knowledge and learning economies. It aspires to build a consistent approach to educational futures in terms of traditional methods, including scenario planning and foresight, as well as imaginative narratives, and it will examine examples of futures research in education, pedagogical experiments, new utopian thinking, and educational policy futures with a strong accent on actual policies and examples.

For Charles and Grace Forde

TABLE OF CONTENTS

PREFACE

This book has arisen from a number of different areas of interest. My original interest lay in the writings of the Women's Peace Movement in which feminist activists and thinkers used a wide variety of utopian and speculative texts to imagine and critique alternative possibilities for the development of a more peaceful and better society. This interest was then developed in my Ph D thesis in which I examined the ideologies of gender in feminist utopian thinking. My more recent involvement in empirical research on issues of gender equality in education raised questions about the polarised debate about the education of boys and girls and about the construction of gender underpinning policy and practice in education. Time and time again, in the analysis of policy and practice, we seemed unable to move beyond a model which sets up the education of boys and girls a two competing sets of needs. In this book then I have returned to my earlier interest in feminist utopian thinking as a means of interrogating the construction of gender in educational policy and practice.

There are a number of people whose support I would like to acknowledge book. Firstly, Michael Peters whose work in setting utopianism in the context of education and educational futures provided me with the frame in which I could adopt the speculative approach to the question of gender and education. This book would not have been possible without Michael's enthusiastic response to my proposal for this speculative approach. I would also like to thank Deborah Cameron for her guidance during the original project on feminism and utopianism. I also owe a debt of gratitude to my fellow colleagues in the Teacher Development Research Group, Alastair McPhee, Margery McMahon and Fiona Patrick who allowed me time away from other projects to complete this book and to the Faculty of Education at the University of Glasgow who supported a period of study leave in which I was able to begin this book. In addition I must acknowledge the readiness of Fiona Patrick and Margery McMahon to read a draft of the book and providing invaluable feedback in bringing together ideas on feminist utopianism and education. Finally, a special note of thanks is due to Linda Cunningham for her continued support.

CHAPTER 1

FEMINIST UTOPIAN THINKING AND THE 'GOOD SOCIETY'

Introduction

Debates on gender in education in western education systems swing from a concern for the education of girls and women to what – in some quarters – has been characterised as a 'moral panic' about the engagement of boys in school education and more recently, in some areas of higher education and within the education professions. However, these discussions have tended to circulate in the popular media around the pattern of the attainment of boys which has changed relative to that of girls in national examinations and this does little to explore the educational experiences and aspirations of girls and boys, women and men within western economically developed democracies. In the midst, then, of this concern expressed both in the media and in educational policy about the attainment of boys, a feminist discussion about the future of educational policy on gender might seem unnecessary. This view must be rebuffed on several counts. Firstly, it is because there is the danger of us moving to a position where the education of girls is once again being eclipsed by concerns about boys' educational attainment – indeed that the progress of some girls is in some way to be the cause of boys' underachievement – that we need to continue to take a critical stance both to current policy and practice and to the formulation of future policy in relation to education and gender. Secondly, we need to consider ways forward that would serve both the interests of girls and boys, women and men. Underlying the statistics are the very different experiences of groups of girls and women, of groups of boys and men: where a range of other social factors such as class, poverty, disability, race, ethnicity and sexuality intersect with gender to powerfully shape educational experiences. We seem to be in danger of moving between two extremes in educational policy and practice: the case for girls/women, the case for boys/men and implicit in each of these cases is the view that, some how one gender 'is to blame' for the lack of progress of the other. The formulation of policy that swings from concerns and initiatives to support the educational progress of girls and women to a crisis about the engagement of boys and young men in education is ultimately to the detriment of both genders, to the educational system and to society as a whole.

Further, we have to also recognise that on a global stage the concern about boys' underachievement relative to that of girls is a 'localised' issue. Globally, women and girls do not readily access education at any level (UNICEF, 2005). Even where primary education is available, social mores, employment and economic structures, religious beliefs and family pressures can lead in practice to many girls being excluded or limited to accessing only a rudimentary education. This has consequences both for the individual and for the wider sociopolitical order. Lack of access to education means girls and women are excluded from other opportunities afforded through educational achievement and this in turn results in the perpetuation of social structures in which girls and women remain subordinate. There is now an urgent need for us to consider alternative approaches to the issue of gender in education. In this book then I look to the debates about gender in the visions of alternative sociopolitical orders found in feminist utopian thinking.

Feminists have used the genre of utopian writing to explore ideas about gender and social change. Feminist utopian writing can be seen as 'a space to speculate' (Wolmark, 1993) where feminists have imagined, constructed and interrogated understandings of gender and the implications of these for the development of the 'good society'; in feminism the 'good society' is defined broadly in terms of the liberation of women but there is considerable variation in how such a society would be structured and how it would be achieved. A critical question explored in these writings is the process by which there could be a 'willed transformation' of society (Williams, 1980) particularly through the agency of women in order to achieve the 'good society'. In utopian writing, education has been constructed as one of the means of bringing about 'the good society' but importantly within feminist utopian writing and thinking what we understand as 'education' is itself being transformed. In feminist utopian thinking, side by side with a critique of formal educational institutions, there is an attempt to think more holistically about the relationship between the educative process and the achievement of women's self-determination both individually and collectively to bring about a realignment of gender relationships in the sociopolitical order. The central purposes of this book are to interrogate the different constructions of gender within feminist utopian thinking and explore critically the implications of these for future educational policy and practice.

Milojevic (2005) suggests that the "…Golden Age of feminist visioning belongs to the second wave of feminism starting in the west in, roughly 1960s and culminating in the 1980s" (p 131). Indeed during this period, a significant body of work was produced generating a range of visions of alternative futures. However, examples of feminist utopian writing cover a much longer historical period. Feminist utopian writing is a substantial but diverse body of work with texts being produced at various points historically when issues related to the position of women in society have come to the fore in the political imagination. This book draws from feminist utopian writing produced over a long historical period; the earliest 'feminist' utopian vision we will look at here is Mary Astell's *A Serious Proposal to the Ladies* which was published in 1696. My intention in examining a range of feminist utopian texts is not to retreat to some nostalgic construction of a golden age of women's education whether in convent of the middle ages, the 'bluestocking' era, the girls' grammar schools of the 1950s and 60s nor even those educational opportunities – formal and informal – fostered in the ferment of the early years of women's liberation. Instead, we can look to these writings to explore issues that continue to be of significance in relation to gender and education today particularly when 'gender fundamentalism' (Kenway, 2004) is becoming prevalent as earlier gender reforms are being derided and dismantled. Further, feminist utopian thinking has continued to develop particularly in discussions associated with 'third wave feminism' (Baumgardener and Richards, 2000) and with 'cyberfeminism' (Hawthorne and Klien, 1997). In both these developments in feminist thought, questions relating to gender have been raised that are of significance to education. It is important to acknowledge the richness of the debate within feminist utopian thinking in relation to both the wider question of the construction of the 'good society' and the more specific issue of the educative process, particularly in the light of the current polarisation of views and consequent educational policy in relation to gender and educational achievement.

The position of this book is feminist, notwithstanding the contested nature of that term and the different positions that co-exist in feminism. It is difficult to discuss 'the feminist position' in relation to education in anything but the very broadest of terms. The discussions in feminism about education are far more wide ranging than is, perhaps, popularly assumed and reflect wider debates about the concept of 'gender' and our understandings of what it means to be a woman/girl. Rather than problematize the diversity of positions in feminism, the intention here is to actively engage with these different positions to consider educational futures in relation to gender and education.

THEORETICAL APPROACH

In this book, I develop an interdisciplinary perspective in order that the diversity of positions in feminism in relation to gender, education and future policy and practice can be explored. I, therefore, need to consider more closely, what is meant by 'interdisciplinary' in the context of this book. The study of women in academic subjects has expanded rapidly since the beginning of second wave twentieth century feminism in the late 1960s. However, problems are created by the bureaucratic organisation of academic institutions where, for example, the study of women in the discipline of psychology becomes separate from discussions about women and the law or women and education. Much of the work is dispersed and diffused across a range of disciplines leading to circumstances where debates and knowledge generated within specific academic disciplines do not come together. The particular focus of this book is to contribute to discussions about gender and educational theory, policy and practice by bringing together different strands to explore the construction of gender in feminist utopian thinking. To do this I draw on ideas from across a range of academic disciplines: psychology, philosophy, sociology, literature, cultural studies as well as education. My intention here is partly echoed in Bowles's (1983) characterisation of the approach to knowledge adopted in Women's Studies: "[o]ur aim is boundary crossing, a move away from this narrow disciplinary specialization (p 40). Notwithstanding this, interdisciplinary approaches can be reduced to an eclectic approach picking up a range of loosely connected ideas, discourses and debates within separate disciplines.

As Coyner (1983) cautions: "[w]e cannot take the research about women willy-nilly from its sources and string it together, expecting the result to be coherent" (p

57). Further, some interdisciplinary approaches can be limiting: interdisciplinary programs and projects do not normally contribute theory and method; they apply theory and method, to solve local 'problems'. To address this criticism Coyner argues for the development of Women's Studies as an academic discipline in its own right" (p 54) and so Coyner continues:

> [w]e may have stumbled on our treasure unaware. We started with concern about sexism. But what we have discovered in women's culture, and what we suspect about the way we will see knowledge itself when we look through our women's eyes, is certainly far bigger than what we expected and far more dramatic" (p 54).

At one level, this proposition is attractive as it helps to delineate the scope and distinctiveness of feminist scholarship as a new academic area. However, such ideas need to be treated with some considerable caution. The notion of 'women's culture' can suggest an essentialist construction of what it means to be a woman: that there are some universal attributes forming the basis of a distinctive women's culture from which to generate knowledge and on which to base a definitive version of an alternative future sociopolitical order. Rather than the construction of a monolithic ideal of what it means to be a woman, what is evident in feminist utopian thinking is the interrogation of a range of positions with regard to the construction of gender.

One of the features of feminist utopian thinking is that feminists have used a variety of disciplines and media to explore, develop and critically appraise alternative sociopolitical orders: feminist utopian thinking can itself be characterised as interdisciplinary. Additionally, one of the features of feminist utopian writing is intertextuality where ideas are shared across not only different disciplines but also different genres of writing with the common enterprise of imagining and analyzing critically alternative sociopolitical orders. Discussions about the development of alternative sociopolitical orders can be seen to be taken up by writers within different disciplines and different forms of writing including literary works, high theory, polemic writings and genre fiction where the common attribute is the speculative quality of the work. Rather than seeking a pre-determined social system, feminists have been able to form, critique and re-form possibilities for a different social order in which women will be liberated. My intention in this book then is not to stitch together in an arbitrary manner a range of diverse ideas into a definitive and seemingly coherent vision of a single educational future but to consider critically visions of alternative sociopolitical orders that have been generated within feminist utopian writing and consider the implications of these for the future development of educational policy and practice. The potential of feminist utopian thinking can be illustrated by examining briefly some classic examples of educational utopias. In these we see the relationship between definitions of what it means to be a person and the educative process in shaping this to achieve an alternative and better society.

EDUCATIONAL UTOPIAS

The term 'utopia' is very much subject to debate. Importantly there is no definitive vision of a 'utopia' but what we have are competing visions of the 'good society'. This diversity is illustrated by McKenna's (2001) development of different models of 'utopia': end state model, anarchist model and a process model and in each of these, education is conceived of differently. The end-state model can be characterized as the aspiration and efforts to achieve the perfect and ideal society. End-state models seek to establish the perfect state and education becomes a form of social conditioning to ensure that inhabitants have those qualities and desires needed to achieve this perfect state. Further, the ideal state becomes one of stasis; all efforts are focused on maintaining the status quo and what follows is the all too easy slide into totalitarianism.

An example of an 'end-state' educational utopia is B.F. Skinner's *Walden Two* (1976) in which he uses the utopian genre to envision the resultant good society created by an alternative form of education emerging from the principles of operant conditioning. In Skinner's (1976) view, for social change,

> what is needed is not a new political leader or a new kind of government but further knowledge about human behavior and new ways of applying that knowledge to the design of cultural practices (p xvi).

Walden Two is intended to explore the social consequences of behavioural engineering. Writing about the publication of this novel in 1948, Skinner indicates that he decided "to write an account of how I thought a group of, say, a thousand people might have solved the problem of their daily lives with the help of behavioral engineering" (p vi) when behavioural engineering was "little more than science fiction" (p vi). What we are provided with in the novel is a vision of a self-sufficient community with a consciously experimental approach to shaping human nature through its educational processes. Frazier, the utopian leader of Walden Two, explains: "we encourage our people to view every habit and custom with an eye to possible improvement" (p 25). Through operant conditioning they have been able to create individuals whose behaviour ensures a harmonious and productive community. The 'curriculum' in the early years of childhood includes controlled problems designed to develop self-control and to motivate children. These are simple, everyday situations but are intentionally constructed to reinforce specific behaviours that conform to the ideals underpinning this community. It was through this form of an educative process based on behaviourist principles that, in Skinner's view, a good society could be developed. However, maintenance of the end-state ideal becomes paramount so any means of attaining this idea is regarded as legitimate and further, any change is deemed as 'degenerative' and must be avoided at all costs.

The second model that McKenna (2001) conceptualises is that of the anarchist model of utopia. Education is no longer constructed as an educational system with formalised authority held by the state but instead is conceived of as a communal and participatory educative process in the hands of the learner. She argues that for this form of education to be established requires a shift in outlook brought about not just by a shift in the material conditions of life but through change in values, beliefs and habits, that is 'transvaluation'. In this the reconstruction of education is not based on 'authority', whether this defined in terms of an individual's power or expertise in a specific area, but instead through communal discussion and debate from which the underpinning premises of the educative process emerge.

Communal discussion is the keynote of A.S. Neill's experimental school Summerhill where all decisions are made at the school meeting at which all pupils as well as teachers can contribute to the process. Summerhill is based on the importance of freedom and the development of happiness. A.S. Neill (1962) argues that though society is faced with enormous social ills, "it does not want ...to lose its sickness" (p 10) having resisted social change and improvement. Neill, continues, that in the current sociopolitical order therefore, "our task as teachers is to fight against a mass psychology" (p 10) where everyone is the same. For him,

> a school that makes active children sit at desks studying mostly useless subjects is a bad school. It is a good school only for those uncreative citizens who want docile, uncreative children who will fit into a civilization whose standard of success is money (p 19-20).

Neill's educational utopia is based on a specific view of human nature in which the child is essentially good not evil and so the core of the educative process is to enable the child to be free. Summerhill could be described, as an anarchist model of an educational utopia in McKenna's terms where there is a radical change in values, beliefs and habits particularly where authority for learning which is located not in the teacher as is traditional but in the child.

McKenna's third model, a process–model of utopia is based on John Dewey's (1966) model of democracy. The realization of an ideal society is not the primary objective but instead the task is one of engaging actively in social experimentation, which requires critical intelligence and which in its turn requires active citizens. Education, therefore, has a central role. One of the aspects of process model utopias is its critical and experimental nature. The critical and experimental characteristics are evident in Robert Owen's intentional utopian communities developed in Great Britain in the early nineteenth century as he and his followers combined socialist and communitarian politics to establish of alternative communities such as New Lanark in Scotland, UK and New Harmony in Indiana, USA. Within Owen's experiments, education played a vital role. As part of his critique of the contemporaneous society, Owen in 'Essays on the Formation of Character: A New View of Society' written between 1813-14, saw two social ills: firstly, most of the population did not have access to education and secondly,

> the far greater part of the remainder of the community are educated upon the most mistaken principles of human nature, such indeed, as cannot fail to produce a general conduct throughout society, totally unworthy of the characters of rational beings (Owen 1968, p 42).

A significant development is evident in Owen's thinking. In New Lanark in Scotland, Owen introduced not just a school but extensive childcare facilities with a clear educational purpose and access to learning for the workers in the mill – both women and men. Though these efforts were enlightened for that period, this was, as Kolmerten (1998) argues, evidence of Owen's "reform-minded benevolent patriarchy" (p16) rather than a radical reconstruction of society. The development of a system of childcare and schooling, for example, was partly intended to reduce the mother's ability to develop 'bad habits' in the child.

When Owen transferred his efforts to other intentional utopian communities in USA and England the goal became one of creating a truly egalitarian utopian society, a central tenet of which was gender equality. By 1824 Owen was involved in the establishment of the utopian community of New Harmony in the USA, at which point, he created "...on paper at least, a blueprint for women's liberation" (Kolmerten 1998, p 27). Owen saw these alternative societies as a way of sweeping aside the three evils of private property, religion and marriage, all of which were obstacles to the achievement of an egalitarian society (Taylor, 1985). In this process model of utopia, the intellectual work of examining critically the experiences within the evolving new sociopolitical order was vital. Debate, discussion, reflection were the driving forces in trying to realise an alternative way of structuring society. Thus in New Harmony education was not limited to a narrow definition of schooling. Instead, education was the formative process by which New Harmony could evolve from being a Preliminary Community – a staging post in the process of social change – into a 'Community of Equality', the utopian community. New Harmony became the gathering point for a number of intellectuals who sought a role in the conceptual development of this experimental society, if not in the day-to-day tasks of sustaining a community. Education involved adults and children of the community as well as the intellectual leaders. Issues and possible alternatives were being constantly debated in the community through lectures given by Owen and others and by the writings in the *New Harmony Gazette*. Although the community was short lived, what is important in Owen's experiments and writings and in the writings of his followers, is the possibility of social change. Further, he highlighted education as one of the means of bringing about social transformation at a point in history when the foundations of an educational system to serve an industrialized economy were being laid which would strengthen a stratified society (Davis, 2006). Owen saw education not as the acquisition of knowledge and skills for work but as a process of character formation arguing that:

> children can be formed collectively to have any human character...they partake of that plastic quality, which by perseverance under judicious management, may be ultimately moulded into the very image of rational wishes and desires (Owen 1968, p 49).

These three examples of different types of utopias illustrate the relationship between utopian thinking and the creation of alternative formations of education.

UTOPIA TODAY

The potential of utopian thinking in helping to generate other possibilities in socio-political policy including educational policy and practice is being recognised today. Two examples of this development are firstly the 'The Real Utopias Project' in the USA and 'Robust Hope Project' (2006) in Australia. 'The Real Utopias' project at the University of Wisconsin is an ongoing project exploring different aspects of social policy. Wright (2005) in his overview of the project argues that "the belief in the possibility of radical alternatives to existing institutions has played an important role in contemporary political life" (hypertext) and the purpose of this project is to "sustain and deepen serious discussion of radical alternatives to existing social practices" (hypertext). The Real Utopias project illustrates the materialist thread of utopianism:

> What we need then, are 'real utopias', utopian ideals that are grounded in the real potentials of humanity, utopian destinations that have accessible waystations, utopian designs of institutions that can inform our practical tasks of muddling through in a world of imperfect conditions for social change (Wright 2005, hypertext).

The project since its inception in 1991 has dealt with a diverse range of topics including 'Deepening Democracy', 'Market Socialism' and 'Gender Egalitarianism in Work and Caregiving'. Education is scheduled to be the focus of a forthcoming project.

Ideas derived from utopian thinking have been developed within a specifically educational context with the Robust Hope project being developed at the University of Western Sydney. Robust Hope is defined as having:

> a futures orientation and a turning away from any sense of hope as something naïve, to a rootedness in evidence based experience. Robust Hope has psychological and sociological dimensions. It affects society and the individual and thus it operates at both a societal and individual level (Whitton 2006, p 13).

The focus of this project is to develop a conceptual tool to examine critically public policy and to allow the generation of policies which can be socially transformative – that is that hope as 'robust hope' is seen as something that can be attained.

These examples of current projects drawing on the tradition of political thought of utopianism where the possibility of willed transformation towards a good or at least better society is held to helps illustrate the potential of utopianism and utopian thought to consider one of the areas in education where current policy seems stuck in a paradigm where the needs of one gender are set against the needs of the other gender. Feminist utopian writings deal specifically with the question of gender and the construction of the 'good society'. In this book we will look to this body of work to explore different ideological constructions of gender and the implications of these ideas for education.

UNDERPINNING IDEAS

As this book takes an interrogatory stance, it is important both to highlight and to problematize some of the key ideas underpinning the discussion. There are three terms embedded within the title of the book that we will examine here in turn in order to outline the focus and position taken in the book:

1. educating for the good society
2. the educative process
3. feminist utopian writing.

EDUCATING FOR THE 'GOOD' SOCIETY

At one level, there is a clear future orientation in an education system that prepares children and young adults for their future lives and roles in society and seeks to enhance the vocational or leisure lives of those adults who later return to education. However, it could be argued that this is preparing the learner to fit into the existing social and political structures. Embedded in the term of 'educating for the good society' is another view of the educational process and the future: education is not simply about reproducing the dominant sociopolitical order but is a means to social and political change. As we have seen with the three examples of educational utopias, there are contrasting ideas of the 'good society' which raise questions of how we define 'good'.

A vision of a 'good society' is clearly value-ladened incorporating the specific ideological position of the creator of that vision. Though the idea of the 'good society' would, in feminist writings, be broadly related to the liberation of women, within this there are some sharp differences based upon contrasting understandings of the construct of 'gender'. Kristeva, (1991) in her influential essay 'Woman's Time' (first published in 1979), identifies three constructions of gender, each of which has a different sociopolitical outcome. Firstly, there is a vision of the good society where sociopolitical structures and systems are established to guarantee women's access to traditional male dominated areas resulting in a society where women gain entry into previously exclusively male arenas. Secondly, there is a vision of the good society which is woman-centred: ideas of femaleness and femininity underpin the sociopolitical order and practices which lead to the predominance of women politically and socially largely in their own separate communities but, in some instances, within the wider society. Thirdly, there is the vision of the good society where gender no longer has any social significance thus potentially creating a gender equal society. Each of these positions has an impact on how we conceive of and conduct the educative process.

THE EDUCATIVE PROCESS

In this book, rather than related more narrowly to the activity of learning within an institutional setting, 'education' is used in its broadest sense as that of the process of human development and growth. Notwithstanding this, the educational system itself is an important aspect. Certainly within the economically developed countries learning from early years into adulthood, including vocational and professional education and learning for leisure all largely takes place within institutional settings. Further, in economically developing countries the expansion of the education system the establishment of western-type models of schools and universities is a pivotal means of pursuing growth within a globalized economy. However, to confine the discussion to education as something that occurs within specific institutions negates the possibility of considering other ways of organising and structuring the formation and learning of both young and adult members of a society. Therefore, it is essential to have as a central idea the notion that education is not simply the state education system that is part of the apparatus of the state through which it can perpetuate itself – whether this system is fully publicly funded, a mixture of public and private or privately funded. Instead, we need to look more broadly at 'educative processes' that will provide us with the means to interrogate current structures and systems and pose alternatives. The educational utopias explored above provide us with an example of the way utopian thinking is experimental. Utopian thinking provides the means to critically appraise the status quo as well as to project and then appraise alternative sociopolitical orders including alternative formations of education.

FEMINIST UTOPIAN THINKING

The term 'feminist utopian thinking' signals another basic premise: that there is a substantial body of work that can be defined as 'feminist utopian thinking'. In their attempts to redefine gender relationships and generate new conceptualisations of gender as the founding ideas of alternative social orders, feminist writers and activists have appropriated two practices derived from utopianism: the establishment of alternative intentional utopian communities and the writing of utopian texts. In the first of these, alternative communities, there have been a number of projects to establish communities based on feminist principles, especially women-only communities. These have been various in design and development – rural communities, protest camps, festival camps, long term, short term (Faderman 1992, Sargisson 2000) – but they are generally perceived as experimental communities with only a limited political and social impact, being outside the lives of the majority of women. The more influential practice has been the production of feminist utopian texts. This, then, leads to the question of how we define feminist utopian writing.

Utopian writing has been regarded by some as a literary form that is no longer relevant to politics today. Krishan Kumar (1987), in his survey of classic utopian writing, argues that a utopian standpoint is no longer viable and utopianism is unable to hold a place on the political agenda or even in the cultural imagination. Thus the utopian impulse, the desire and anticipation of a better society in the future, is replaced by an anti-utopian stance which denies the possibility of social improvement. The only acceptable approaches are either to maintain society as it is currently structured or give way to a nihilist despair: an anti-utopian stance is, therefore, inherently and deeply conservative. Consequently, Kumar argues that significant utopian texts that have the political impact that, for instance, Edward Bellamy's (1982) *Looking Backwards* had when it was published in 1881, are no longer being produced. Instead, Kumar concentrates predominantly on 'classic' male authored utopian texts and sees texts written in the 1930s and 1940s like Aldous Huxley's *Brave New World* (1932) and George Orwell's *1984* (1949) as exemplars of anti-utopia, the dominant mode of utopianism within the twentieth century. Kumar acknowledges that utopianism does still exist, manifested in both social theory and alternative lifestyles, but he regards these works as marginal:

> There has even been an interesting revival of the utopian novel among certain contemporary groups, as among the feminists. But this serves only to underline the weakness of utopia as a central symbol, capable of evoking a response from society as a whole (p 420).

However, Kumar's criticism of feminist utopian writings as minor works has much to do with the politics of production (many of the works published in the 1970s and 1980s were published by independent feminist presses) and a continuing view that gender politics is a minority concern. Others scholars do not share Kumar's view of feminist utopian writing and its significance in the process of sociopolitical change.

In his studies of contemporary utopian writing *Demand the Impossible* (1986) and *Scraps of the Untainted Sky* (2000), Tom Moylan suggests a new utopian phase is evident from the mid 1970s with the publication of novels such as *The Female Man* (1974/75) by Joanna Russ. He argues that these texts, which he describes as 'critical utopias', stem from the liberatory politics of the late 1960s and 1970s and are distinct from previous utopian works.

"The new novels negated the negation of utopia by the forces of the twentieth century history: the subversive imaging of utopian society and the radical negativity of dystopian perception is preserved; while the systematizing boredom of traditional utopia and the cooptation of utopia by modern structures is destroyed. Thus, utopian writing in the 1970s was saved by its own destruction and transformation into the 'critical utopia'" (p 10). Among the 'critical utopias', cited by Moylan, feminist novels form the largest group. Feminist utopian writing has played a significant political role in the politics of gender.

The use of utopian writing as a forum of debate has been of critical importance in the development of thinking about the nature of the good society within contemporary feminism. Of the various movements that emerged during the late 1960s, the feminist movement is distinctive in the production of a substantial body of work within the genre of utopian writings in which visions of the 'good society' are constructed and interrogated. In producing this work there is a clear political end. What we can see is the use of the utopian genre by feminists at particular historical moments to explore contemporaneous issues in relation to the position of women. We can see within each of these moments that the question of the education of girls and women is a concern. However, the formation of education itself is not an unchanging idea as equally the educative process reflects the concerns of that moment: what is deemed appropriate education for women/girls, men/boys will rest on an understanding of the concept of 'gender'.

The term 'feminist utopian writing' might suggest clear coherence and a tradition. However, as we will discuss in the next chapter, it is difficult to define 'feminist utopian writing' in terms of literary features or as a continuous tradition of writing. Instead, we are dealing with a more diverse set of texts, the common feature being the intent of the author to contribute through speculative writing (Barr 1987, 1993) – fictional and non-fictional – to debates about gender and the sociopolitical order. In these texts, the idea of 'utopia' as a good or at least better place is fore grounded but at the same time problematized. It is this idea of utopia which is a primary concern of this study in which we look to these critical utopias to explore the issue of gender and education. In the discussion, so far the term 'utopia' has been used in a variety of ways. At this point, then, it would be useful to define this and related terms.

UTOPIA, EUTOPIA AND DYSTOPIA

The term 'utopia' coined by Thomas More (1976) in his literary work *Utopia* first published in 1516, from two Greek words 'eu' meaning 'no' and 'topos' meaning 'place'. Originally, the term 'utopia' signified that the imaginary alternative social order was better than the contemporaneous society, as is the case in Thomas More's text. However, the term 'utopia' is now used both to describe a better society and in a more general sense to describe any alternative society regardless of the quality of this society. Subsequently, a number of other terms have been generated to distinguish different types of societies – imaginary or real – particularly the terms 'eutopia' and 'dystopia'. In this book the term 'utopia' is used in the broader sense to refer to an alternative society regardless of quality and, following Sargent (1975), the terms 'eutopia' and 'dystopia', are used to indicate the type of alternative society. 'Eutopia' is used to describe a good or at least a better social order than the contemporaneous society which has not previously existed, and 'dystopia' is used to describe a society worse than the contemporaneous society and which, again, has not existed in the past. Dystopia is a nightmare society which extrapolates from and takes to extremes certain trends in contemporary society to provide a warning and to prompt action to bring about the necessary changes for the establishment of a eutopia.

The playfulness of More's original neologism continues to be exploited as new words are generated to suggest different perspectives. Terms such as 'ecotopia', 'heterotopia and 'cybertopia' each signal specific concerns about the process of social transformation. The first term has been derived from the title of Ernest Callenbach's (1975) fictional utopian text, *Ecotopia* in which the utopian figure is a society based firmly on the principles of ecology politics, the second, 'heterotopia' derived from Michael Foucault's lecture 'Of Other Spaces' (1984) and used by Samuel Delaney in an appendix to his novel *Triton* (1992) to emphasize plurality rather than conformity as the distinctive feature in the construction of alternative communities, the third 'cybertopia' signals debates around the impact of digital technologies on the sociopolitical order and the possibility of constructing a 'good society' in the virtual world of cyberspace. The continued generation of ideas is evident in the latest term to be generated which is particularly relevant to this book, that of 'edutopias' (Peters and Freeman-Moir, 2006) in which alternative educational futures can be created and critiqued. My intention in this book is to look to feminist utopian thinking to consider alternative futures in relation to gender and education.

AN OVERVIEW OF THE BOOK

This book is divided into two sections. In the first section I outline the discussions in relation to the two key concepts within this study, that of 'utopianism' and that of 'gender'. Thus in chapter two I examine the debates about utopianism and utopian thinking with the intention of demonstrating the potential of feminist utopian thinking to contribute to thinking on educational futures. In chapter three the role feminist utopian thinking has played in the development of the education for women and girls is then explored by discussing some examples of early feminist utopian works. In chapter four I examine different ideologies of gender which can be found in feminist utopian writing to provide a framework to explore different ideological positions found in feminist utopian thinking with regard to gender.

In the second section of the book, the focus turns to examining specific themes emerging from these discussions of utopia and gender and to considering the implications of these themes in education. Chapter five explores the debates about women's distinctiveness and the implications of these for the construction of knowledge and of pedagogy within education. Chapter six examines the significance of the task of mothering within feminist utopian thinking, and the possibilities of constructing education as a nurturing relationship mirroring that of mother and child. Chapter seven focuses on the issue of technology and gender in particularly in cyberfeminist utopian discussions and again considers how these might shape educational policy and practice. Chapter eight looks to the debates about diversity and intersectionality in the utopian writings that are emerging from 'third wave feminism' (Heywood and Drake, 1997), a term used broadly to describe the feminism of a younger generation of women and considers the possibilities of 'gender free' education.

Historically, there are examples of utopian writing and of intentional utopian communities that have provided alternative visions of education. Feminism can be characterized as a utopian discourse and practice which has helped to question purposes and practices within the current structures and activities of the educational system. In this book the key focus is on looking to feminist utopian thinking as a means of developing a visionary analysis of gender and education. In the next chapter we turn to the idea of 'feminist utopian thinking' and explore how this has enabled feminists to move beyond the analysis of the status quo and explore alternative sociopolitical orders.

CHAPTER 2

FEMINISM AND UTOPIA

Introduction

The place of utopianism and utopian thinking in education has been the subject of recent discussions (Peters and Freeman-Moir 2006, Milojevic, 2005, Halpin, 2003a). There are historical examples of educationalists using this genre of writing to examine education, for instance B.F. Skinner's *Walden Two* (1976) which we examined in the previous chapter as well as examples of education being a cornerstone of intentional utopian communities such as those established by Robert Owen (1968) in the nineteenth century. However, it is too limiting to focus solely on examples where an educationalist has used one of the utopian practices – writing or the establishment of an intentional community – to examine the educative process. Instead we can draw from a much more substantial body of work, both scholarly and popular, exploring utopianism and utopian communities and with studies in a variety of disciplines such as politics, sociology, history or literature. Utopianism with its connotations of 'unrealistic', 'fantasy' or 'totalitarianism' might seem distant from the lived experiences of educators and learners but there are many points at which education and utopianism connect. Both the critical and the imaginative impulses within utopianism help us to conceive of alternatives because "... at its core [is] a powerfully materialist impulse directly concerned with the conditions in which human societies and human individuals might maximise happiness and fulfilment" (Davis 2006, p 592). For those concerned with educational futures there is much to be gained from exploring imaginary societies in a wide range of utopian texts, where education is not only fundamental to the construction of the sociopolitical order but where the educative process is treated to critical examination and alternatives paradigms considered.

We need to consider the contribution of 'utopian thinking', what Halpin (2003a) calls "the utopian imagination" (p 2), in education and the generation of different constructions of the 'good society' can contribute to the development of new visions of the educative process. Though feminist utopian writings – like other utopian texts – might be perceived as simply fanciful or unrealistic visions, feminist utopian thinking provides the means of critiquing the present and offering alternative possibilities particularly around issues of gender. Milojevic (2005) highlights the potential and importance of utopian thinking in education both to critique the present through the lens of a utopian discourse and to put forward alternatives. Citing Grosz (1990), Milojevic argues that to solely criticize without alternatives implies that there are no alternatives to the hegemonic order, which perpetuates the view that the current arrangements must be the right and 'natural' forms. To appreciate why feminist utopian thinking can make a significant contribution to educational policy and practice in relation to gender, firstly, I explore utopianism as a tradition of political thought and the nature of 'utopian thinking' and secondly, I examine issues related to feminist utopianism and writing.

UTOPIANISM AS A TRADITION OF POLITICAL THOUGHT

Utopianism is a tradition in political thought but a precise definition of utopianism is difficult for a number of reasons. Firstly, definitions of both utopianism and utopian writings have tended to be based largely on Thomas More's neologism used in the title of his literary text *Utopia* (1967) and because of this association with More's fictional work, utopianism is often seen as unrealistic or fanciful or situated outside mainstream society and not directly challenging the dominant culture. Thus 'utopianism' is reduced to a sense of hopefulness part of a natural optimism for a better world. When the term 'utopianism' is used to represent a genre of writing, there are also difficulties in seeking a simple definition. There are examples of this form of writing reaching back to classical literature and can also be found in speculative fiction (Barr, 1987, 1992 and 1993) including science fiction utopias and cybertopias (Milojevic, 2005).

When utopianism is used to describe a particular political position it tends to be associated with a specific set of political philosophies and movements that reached their height during the nineteenth century. They include Owenite socialism which we looked at previously, developed by Robert Owen in Great Britain and the USA in the 1820s, the communitarian movements through which a number of utopian settlements were established in both Europe and the USA and the philosophies and social experiments developed by Charles Fourier and Claude Henri Saint-Simon in France. This form of 'utopian' socialism was rejected by Engels and Marx in favour of 'scientific' socialism and consequently is sometimes seen as having little relevance to contemporary politics. However utopianism can be viewed as a more extensive tradition the central focus of which is the struggle to establish an ideal or at social and political contexts.

As a tradition of political thought, utopianism tends to be only intermittently at the forefront of the political agenda and imagination, coming into play at periods of historical disjuncture or rapid social change, for example, evolving social and political structures during the sixteenth century, the coming of industrialisation in the nineteenth century and the wave of liberation politics of the 1960s and 1970s. Thus as Williams (1980) argues, the content of utopian thought is vastly changeable and ideas about a good or at least a better society and there is the possibility that these visions may be accommodated within the dominant discourses rather than used to develop an oppositional ideology as they are today. We can see this tendency to accommodate radical ideas in contemporary society.

The hegemonic culture (Gramsci, 1971) – for example, western patriarchal capitalism- deals with the utopian ideal of a better society in two distinct ways.

Firstly, any practice derived from utopianism can be positioned as a peripheral and often illegitimate alternative: experimental communes are constructed as subversive and utopian writings as minor works of fantasy. Alternatively, women's hopes, for example, of an improved position in a fairer society can be co-opted into the dominant discourses by transforming these hopes into the desires of the individual, fulfilment of which can only be achieved within the dominant value systems. Examples of this are readily available, for instance, ideas of a more equitable society where health care and leisure pursuits for women are seen as important, are converted into individual desires which will be fulfilled by the products and values of the dominant order: a better life will be found through the latest diet or exercise video. Traditional definitions of femininity continue to be circulated through these products; not only is women's behaviour circumscribed but there is an attempt to co-opt their desires into the values of patriarchal capitalism.

Similarly, ideas of a good or at least fairer society, where education for women and girls is seen as a core right, are converted into the ambitions of individual – frequently privileged – women accessing educational opportunities because of their singular standing: as a privileged or 'bright' woman. One woman's success or the success of a small group of privileged women does not necessarily change the circumstances and opportunities of all women and girls. The singular status of these women in which they are marked out as 'unusual' allows the continued circulation of hegemonic definitions of femininity. Not only does access to all areas of education by women and girls remain circumscribed but also aspirations are coopted into the dominant ideas of what it means to be a woman. If utopianism is simply elided with a desire (rather than action) for a better world, which in turn is defined in terms of individual betterment, then there is a deeply conservative outcome.

Utopianism, nevertheless, is a tradition of political thought that has been influential in a range of movements seeking to bring about significant sociopolitical change within western democratic society and has now been appropriated by feminism. We need to separate out the use of the utopian ideal of 'a better society' in the formulation of an oppositional ideology that focuses on the transformation of society, from the way in which this ideal can be used to maintain the dominant ideologies. Rather than try to delineate the content of utopianism, we need to focus on the way in which ideas of social improvement operate. Mannheim's (1954) crucial distinction between ideology and utopia enables us to consider 'utopia' as an oppositional construct that challenges the dominant discourses: both utopia and ideology transcend reality, but whereas ideology provides coherence to a set of existing social and political relationships, the function of utopia is "... to burst the bonds of the existing order..." (p 173). The resulting 'wish-images' become alternatives in terms both of ideas and of political action and, in doing so, assert the imaginative element of utopianism and its relevance to actual political movements where a set of radical political principles inform the establishment of alternative social orders. Mannheim underlines the importance of utopia not just as a vision of a better society but also as an impetus to actual change that people will actively try to bring about.

The central concept of utopianism is, as Williams (1980) suggests, in the idea of 'willed-transformation', the notion that a better society can be created by the agency of members of the existing society. This sense of the possibility of another more perfect world existing elsewhere has been, as Manuel and Manuel (1979) argue, a significant cornerstone of Western Christian thought and, indeed, Kumar (1987) argues that it is unique to this cultural tradition. Kumar regards constructs of other worlds found in non-Christian cultures as paradisical myths in which a perfect world is achieved through the agency of the deity. This viewpoint has been challenged by Sargisson (1996) who proposes that conceiving utopian texts as simply a phenomenon in Christian western culture brings "…the danger of cultural imperialism and exclusivity" (p 13). She cites Sargent's (1994) essay in which he notes that "…utopias are not solely the product of the Christian west, but utopias as a genre of literature that has certain formal characteristics are most common in the West, almost certainly because the genre is identified with Thomas More, a person from the Christian west" (quoted by Sargisson, p 14). What this discussion does point to is the important distinction between wishful thinking, religious beliefs and the possibility of change through political action. Within Western culture, which draws simultaneously from classical philosophy and Judeo-Christian theology, we find the central notion of utopianism this 'willed-transformation' of society, that is social change to be achieved through political action.

The idea that change is both desirable and possible is pivotal in utopianism but we are still left with the problem of the variability in the subject matter of this tradition. Jameson (2005) in the opening of his latest work on utopianism, *Archaeologies of the Future*, highlights the tensions evident in the concept of 'utopia' both as a literary genre and as a tradition of political thought:

> Utopia has always been a political issue, an unusual destiny for a literary form: yet just as the literary value of the form is subject to permanent doubt, so also its political status is structurally ambiguous. The fluctuations of its historical context do nothing to resolve its variability, which is also not a matter of taste or individual judgement (p xi).

As Jameson notes, both as a tradition of political thought and as a literary genre, considerable debate surrounds the constructs of 'utopianism' and 'utopia'. Notions of what constitutes the good or better society are themselves ideologically constructed and depend upon specific political positions. The contrast, for example, between Plato's (1987) 'utopian' vision of a strictly ordered hierarchical society in *The Republic* and the visions of egalitarian societies found within the work and writings of nineteenth century utopian socialists such as Robert Owen (1968) marks a tension between theories concerning the nature of utopian thought (that is the 'willed-transformation' component) and the political ideologies that are viewed as having a utopian intent (generally now equated with more egalitarian ideologies). Consequently, building on Mannheim's definition of utopia, the discussion has turned to the function of utopian thought rather than the content.

UTOPIAN THINKING

As a result of the difficulties of delineating utopianism as a specific ideology, Bloch, (1986) in his work *The Principle of Hope*, seeks to politicise the sense of hopefulness (termed 'the utopian propensity') that social improvement by human agency is both possible and desirable by linking this sense of agency within the political process of change rather than with any one specific political ideology. He argues that utopianism is not an attempt to create alternatives outside society but instead is part of the transformation of contemporary society towards the 'Not Yet'.

This concept of the 'Not-Yet' enables Bloch to counter the problems brought about by the frequent conflation of utopianism with individual desires. It also helps him to address the paradox of utopia: utopia must be always something to be anticipated because once utopia is achieved it is no longer utopia. Nevertheless, utopia must not remain at the level of hopes and within Bloch's schema, he divides the 'Not-Yet' into the 'Not-Yet-Conscious' and the 'Not-Yet-Become'. Whereas 'The Not-Yet Conscious' denotes the ideas that are not yet formed in thought, but are simply desires for improvement, the 'Not-Yet-Become' are the formed ideas which have yet to be realised materially. As Moylan (1986) argues, in this distinction between 'conscious' and 'become', Bloch highlights the anticipatory function of utopia as a subjective experience, but also holds out the possibility of the political achievement of utopian outcomes by transcribing these desires and aspirations into a political agenda. In doing so, Bloch indicates the political importance of the subjective experience and the articulation of this in a public forum in order to move towards the possibility of social transformation.

Bloch's lack of attention to content, however, does return us to the possibility of the utopian ideal being co-opted by the dominant order. We need some way in which we can identify the process by which longing for a better future can be affirmed and transformed into a radical political process, a framework provided to some degree by Marcuse (1966) who links utopianism to ideas of freedom as a necessary part of the process of social change. In 'The End of Utopia' (1970), Marcuse, writing at a time of significant social upheaval – the 1960s –-argues that technological changes are bringing the possibility of radical change in the process of production and labour and in the construction of subjective experience:

> What is at stake is the idea of a new theory of man [sic], not only as theory but also as a way of existence: the genesis and development of a vital freedom and of the vital needs of freedom – of a freedom no longer based on and limited by scarcity and the necessity of alienated labour (1970, p 65).

It is through the notion of utopia that we can begin to construct the possibility of a radically transformed social order. Utopia provides the means at least of imagining the possibility of an oppositional set of values held both collectively and subjectively and the subsequent imagining of these in a social framework: utopia, which is here elided with freedom, does not exist yet but we should be assured of the possibility of its achievement. Marcuse's play on the term 'utopian' and the merging of two seemingly contradictory meanings of utopia, as impossible and as a negation of the dominant values, emphasises not only the profundity of the social transformation being sought but also suggests its potential achievement.

UTOPIA AND HOPE IN EDUCATION

Kumar (1987) argues that against the backdrop of war, pending nuclear and ecological disaster the utopian perspective has given way to an anti-utopian stance which denies the possibility of social and political improvement. However, not only in feminism and other radical movements of the late twentieth century is a utopian stance is evident, but more recently in discussions about social policy, Bloch's (1986) idea of the utopian propensity is evident. The importance of a sense of hopefulness that change is possible is recognised in efforts to bring about social improvement. Halpin (2003a), in his book *Hope and Education* looks at the role of utopian thinking, 'the utopian imagination' in education by drawing from a range of writers who either work within or comment on utopianism to put the case for utopian thinking contributing to the development of educational policy and practice. In looking at hope in education Halpin makes a distinction similar to that of Bloch's: the 'Not-Yet Conscious' and the 'Not-Yet-Become'. Thus, hope can be either wistful thinking, a nebulous yearning or 'ultimate hope'. Drawing from Marcel (1951) and Godfrey (1987), Halpin defines ultimate hope as 'aimed hope' that has specific social objectives. Halpin sees 'ultimate hope' as vital for education because it guards against such views as despair, cynicism and an over regard for tradition. We have seen, in the previous chapter, a similar idea being taken up in the 'Robust Hope' project at the University of Western Sydney.

In seeking solutions to endemic social problems or, in this case, educational issues, utopian thinking can offer ways of constructing creative solutions. Beck's (1977) critique of the dominant tendency in doctrinaire politics – 'Either/Or' politics – to stress one solution and make the case for this by rejecting all other possibilities is important here. Halpin draws from Giddens (1994) as well as Beck, in putting forward the case for ultimate hope in education aligning utopian thinking and the move to 'a third-way' in social policy and politics. The augmentative and sometimes combative form of politics that dominates today disallows creativity in the task of seeking alternatives. Utopian thinking is one means of: "finding a new politics of education that is differently political to the ways most of us have grown used – one that side-steps earlier antagonism in favour of a new pragmatic eclectism" (p 8). To counter the effects of the dominant 'Either-Or' form of politics, Halpin proposes that we should be seeking integrated solutions which bring together experimental ideas which may reflect very different ideological origins but which relate to the problems and circumstances facing society today. He sees Anthony Giddens's form of utopian realism – the third way (Giddens, 1998) – as a way of developing a new politics of education that is removed from the Either/Or. Halpin argues that the third way:

> [u]ndoubtedly encourages critical reflection on the limitations of the here and now and on ways to improve them. As such [it] offers a model exercise in both asking and prompting the asking of questions…[The third way] is not to provide a new totalizing analysis, but to offer a

> heuristic framework within which alternatives can be generated and their relative merits deliberated (p 355).

A similar theme is evident in John Dewey's writings of the 1930s. In John Dewey's extensive body of work, there is a clear future orientation and in a number of texts he examines the relationship between education and democracy (Dewey's definition of a 'good' society) where critical foresight is central. In Dewey's view we must try to develop the society we aspire to by applying critical intelligence to the present and working towards this society. McKenna (2001) argues that "this ongoing process of making the future is what Dewey calls "lived experience" (p 84); whereas received experience is about accepting passively the current situation, lived experience has a future orientation. By critically engaging with and examining our experience, we can seek to improve this world. Dewey calls such goals, 'ends-in-view' (p 86). However, these 'ends-in-view' are not static like the goals of the end-state model of utopia as defined by McKenna but these will be continuous chains of 'ends-in-view' which are dynamic. In this, McKenna argues that:

> [w]e must recognize the indeterminate nature of the future and realize the impact of our individual and societal choices upon it. We must accept responsibility for creating the future, develop a critical method of directing it, and not wait for it to unfold separately from us (p 86).

Therefore, for Dewey education is the process by which we can achieve a better future both individually and societally. Education is the means of creating the critical faculties necessary for individuals to experiment and to reflect on various and changing 'ends-in-view'. There is a question though of how realistic must these alternatives, the 'ends-in-view', must be to the day-to-day realities of education.

UTOPIAN REALISM

Halpin (2003b) regards current work in seeking new or alternative formations of education as a form of utopian realism. In his comparison of Tim Brighouse's work as London Schools Commissioner and his writings on comprehensive schools with that of Thomas More, Halpin describes their shared stance as:

> a militant optimism of will allied to a wish to describe in detail what a better way of living might look like, implying the important necessity to seek out utopian visions to guide social policy and public practice when each is failing miserably to live up to the high ideals we have for them (2003b, p 12).

However, the term 'utopian realism' is a clear contradiction and there is an issue whether utopian thinking can provide workable solutions and indeed, whether this is desirable. Levitas (2004) is critical of Halpin's (2003a) use of utopianism to look at educational policy. In her view, Levitas regards the utopian hope Halpin discusses as being ambushed "...by pragmatism and reduced to materialism" (p

273). She argues instead for the importance of the imaginative, disruptive element of utopianism "[t]hat fancifulness, imagination, desire for a different life, ability to see beyond the constraints of the present and hope for a better world that characterises utopianism" (p 273). Levitas also points up an intrinsic paradox of utopia: once utopia is achieved, it can no longer be utopia, that is 'no place' so there always needs to be an element of work in progress. Part of the power of utopian thinking is its function in helping us imagine other sociopolitical orders but there is an additional dimension when we are look to utopianism in education. Utopianism helps us to consider not just possible alternative futures but the process of sociopolitical change and the agency of individuals and groups in achieving this.

Thus we have on the one hand, Halpin's use of utopian thinking to examine specific contemporary concerns in education. He, for example, explores issues related to school governance, leadership and management and the curriculum through the lens of utopian thinking. On the other hand, Levitas highlights the more open-ended and playful dimension of utopian thinking which ferment disjunctures and fissures through which other previously inconceivable ideas are formed. There is then the question of whether these two positions are reconcilable. A short essay, 'Dewey Outlines Utopian Schools' might seem to fulfil Halpin's ambitions for utopian thinking in which Dewey (1933) provides an account of an alternative form of education in which there is not only a sense of hope of change for the better but there is a formation of education that could be realistically achieved. In this essay, Dewey presents a vision of an alternative and better educational system in Utopia. There are not schools but "assembly places" (p 136) where children and older adults come together to engage in learning. Participation is a vital aspect of learning in this setting and so there is a limit of two hundred on the number of people gathered together in these assembly places is 200, any more could not support "close intimate personal acquaintance" (p 136) on which the educative process is based. Instead of traditional classrooms, learning is conducted through practical tasks in workshops or through cross generational educational groups using an apprentice model of learning: "the adult leaders, through their previous experience and by the manner of their selection, combine special knowledge of children with special gifts in certain directions" (p 137).

In this essay, Dewey is able to critique the dominant model of education based on the acquisition of knowledge and skills and propose instead the purpose should be the development of the positive capacities of each learner.

> This attitude which resulted in a sense of positive power involved, of course, elimination of fear, of embarrassment, of constraint, of self-consciousness. Eliminated the conditions which created the feeling of failure and incapacity. Possibly, it included the development of confidence, of readiness to tackle difficulties, of actual eagerness to seek problems instead of dreading them and running from them. It included a rather ardent faith in human capacity (p 146).

To read Dewey's essay, however, as simply a plan for an alternative educational system limits its potential as an exercise in creative thinking. The essay neatly encapsulates the idea of utopian thinking as form of experimental thinking in which Dewey has generated a possible way of forming education to achieve democracy, (Dewey's construction of the 'good society'). The move from the acquisition of knowledge to the formation of attitudes reflects the move from "an acquisitive economic society" (p 139) to a society where not just individual happiness and fulfilment are its goals but also includes the creation of a genuinely participatory democratic society.

Dewey's essay illustrates that we need not polarize the positions, of firstly, Halpin (2003b) who seeks to develop utopian realism and Levitas (2004) who emphasises the experimental nature of utopian thinking. Instead, it is more constructive, in relation to the purposes of this discussion on gender in education, to see these as part of a continuum where the role of utopian thinking is to illuminate and critique the material reality of education today by posing alternatives which may be more or less 'real', more or less realisable.

Feminists inherit the traditions of utopian political thought because within feminism there is an emphasis on the transformation of society through the agency of women to achieve a better society for themselves and others. Utopianism, then, offers feminists the means not only to challenge patriarchal ideologies but further, by looking imaginatively beyond the perimeter of contemporary patriarchal society and postulating other and better societies based on feminist principles, to articulate coherently oppositional ideologies. In feminist utopian thinking, we see this range of visions of alternative societies from more architectural blueprints of the change process to more imaginative creations. The purpose of these alternative visions is to reveal the underlying ideologies which seek to naturalise and sustain current social formations by denying the possibility of alternatives often drawing on the feature of fantasy or science fiction utopian forms. These visions, whether more 'realistic' or more 'fantastic', help to reveal the workings of dominant ideologies of gender in education, as well as importantly proposing the possibility of alternatives – the sense of hope fundamental to social improvement.

FEMINIST UTOPIANISM

The idea that there is a 'feminist' utopianism has been examined in depth by Lucy Sargisson (1996). Feminism, for Sargisson, has a "...utopian potential. It is rooted in dissatisfaction with the present. It comes from an estranged, alienated perspective and, as such, it creates spaces in which we can think differently about the world" (p 25). In the light of feminism, Sargisson attempts to reconceptualize what is meant by utopianism. Sargisson, like a number of writers previously, disputes the common usage of 'utopia' as the perfect state. In her view, recent expressions of utopianism, particularly from contemporary second and third wave feminism (including both fiction and non-fictional texts as well as other aesthetic forms), have rejected notions of death or closure. Sargisson also questions Mannheim's (1954) dichotomy of the 'critical' and the 'utopian' because central to Mannheim's explanation is the assumption that utopianism anticipates reality which is, she suggests, a view that reduces utopianism almost to the level of being a 'blueprint for the future'. Instead utopianism in Sargisson's view is akin to that of

Levitas (2004) emphasising the more complex and open ended nature of utopianism in the functioning of: "… the most radical function as new and different social arrangements can be best imagined in a space free from the constraints, norms and codes of present society" (p 50).

Sargisson importantly moves the debate from seeking a single 'true' alternative to emphasizing the open-ended nature of utopianism and so we should be more concerned with multiplicity of ideas than with definitive solutions. Thus, utopianism in its current manifestations particularly in feminism is concerned with debates about the construction of meaning. The process of speculating about the possibility of an ideal or better society brings with it criticism of the dominant order, which is sometimes implicit, but more often, explicitly stated. Utopianism allows feminists to criticize the current sociopolitical structures as well as providing the means of speculating and experimenting with alternative cultural definitions. Although this speculation might seem to have little relevance to the material struggles of feminism and the quest for an equal educative process, it is a vital dimension in any political and social transformation. There is a strong parallel between what Bloch is advocating in relation to the 'Not Yet Become' as the basis of a politics of social transformation and the feminist approach which has been to politicize women's personal experiences and turn these into goals within a process of social change: 'the personal is political' (Hanisch, 2000).

In feminism, the process of willed-transformation is both a material and an ideological process. Feminist thought, has, as Eisenstein (1984) suggests, "...an element of visionary, futurist thought..." (p xiv) in which there is clearly the sense of hopefulness Bloch sees as the precursor of social improvement. This utopian propensity provides feminist theorists with the means of developing a speculative approach in the search for a distinctively new society in which women are no longer subjugated. It also enables feminist theorists to examine issues related to the social and political structure of a new society and the discursive practices that would underpin this society. If we are to envision a better educative process in which women and men, boys and girls can thrive then we need to go beyond current ideologies. Sargisson (1996) also notes the diversity of forms and practices – literary, aesthetic, and practical – in utopian thinking as well as diversity in content and so stresses the importance of function. Rather than characterize utopianism as the development of 'utopias', that is a plan of idealized alternative sociopolitical orders, Sargisson emphasises the possibilities of utopian thinking: "transgressive utopianism" (p 24) can change the ways we think.

FEMINIST UTOPIAN WRITING

There are examples of feminist utopian writing over a long period but it is difficult to propose that there is a tradition of feminist writing because historically utopian works by women have been lost to the subsequent generations. From the work of literary critics such as Kessler (1984), Albinski (1988), Barkowski (1989) and Burwell (1997) there appear to be both periods in which a substantial number of utopian texts are produced by women, tending to coincide with periods when issues relating to women are significant, and periods of inactivity – both in terms of political action related to women's issues and utopian writing – in which the works of previous generations are neglected. Thus, what we see at particular historical moments, when the position of women in society is a predominant theme in the political imagination, is the use of utopian writing to critically explore future alternatives. When a significant issue in relation to the position of women in society becomes a dominant theme in the cultural imagination, the utopian genre provides women – and some men – with a forum in which they can contribute to this debate. The early twentieth century was one such period of activity (first wave feminism) the period beginning in the early 1970s is another (second wave feminism) and we have now the emergence of third wave feminism from approximately the mid-1990s.

In their use of the genre as a forum for political debate, feminist writers have also transformed it (Moylan, 1986). With its roots in More's Utopia, traditionally utopian writing has been regarded as a literary genre. However, if we look at the body of work within feminist utopian writing – it is very diverse in form. Feminist utopian writing includes fictional and non-fictional writing, and within each of these, further diversity of form is evident. In non-fictional writings, we move from ephemeral works such as manifestos, to polemic writings to works of high theory. Similarly, with fictional feminist writing, we move from works which have become part of the literary canon (albeit some of these texts have had to be reclaimed by this generation) to genre fiction. Critically important here is the idea of 'intertextuality'. Looking at this diverse body of work, ideas about the 'good or better society' are explored and interrogated across texts. There are borrowings across fiction and non-fiction feminist utopian texts and it is this permeability of the boundary that adds to the significance of these works as a forum for debate within feminism.

Given this diversity, there is a question about how we define a utopian text as 'feminist'. Kessler, in her efforts to reclaim early examples of women's utopian writing in the USA, cites several criteria for classifying a text as 'feminist' which stand up to scrutiny in the light of contemporary understandings of the concept 'feminist'. Utopian texts are deemed 'feminist' if they "... provide a critique of women's status, offer alternative ways of being female, recommend reforms benefiting women, place women centrally in the plot, show either sex atypically..." (p 21). Of these criteria, perhaps the only one not fully clear is "...alternative ways of being female..." but from the discussion of specific texts, Kessler appears to be using this criterion to describe changes in traditional gender roles rather than arguing that there is a female experience essentially different from a male experience. These criteria very much focus on the ideological stance embedded in the content of a particular text and resemble what is suggested by Joanna Russ (1981) in her study of feminist utopian novels produced in the 1970s: "... the works form a remarkably coherent group in their presentation of feminist concerns and the feminist analyses which are central to these concerns" (p 71).

Content and the ideological stance are significant aspects in the delineation of feminist utopian writing and these are criteria that can be applied to both literary novels and genre fiction. We need to define contemporary feminist utopian texts not only in terms of the philosophical ideas upon which the constructs of a better society are based, as Kessler (1984) and Russ (1981) propose, but also in terms of their political functioning which is developed through a specific aesthetic practice. The philosophical, political and aesthetic aspects of these texts come together in the sense of displacement or 'estrangement' experienced by the reader which is a central aspect of Suvin's (1979) influential definition of utopian works: "Utopia is the verbal construction of a particular quasi-human community where institutions, norms and individual relationships are organised according to a more perfect principle than the author's community, this construction being based on estrangement arising out of an alternative historical hypothesis" (p 49). The reader of feminist utopian writing is challenged by a plausible alternative found in the text in which traditional gender relationships are restructured in some way, and so she can begin to confront the structures and values underpinning patriarchal society. Many works of genre fiction such as science fiction utopias, fantasy, 'sword and sorcery' and romance utopias also meet this criterion of estrangement.

Suvin's definition is typically applied to fictional works. However, Angelika Bammer (1991) and Lucy Sargisson (1996) both argue that fictional utopian writing should be placed in the wider field of feminist utopianism. Although Bammer argues that in feminism the utopian imagination has been most frequently expressed through fictional texts, she relates the production of some of the fictional utopian works to developments within the Women's Liberation Movement. Further, these works are contributing to the development of the specific tradition of feminist utopian thinking. Sargisson also has a different starting point from many of the studies by literary scholars. She views the phenomenon of utopianism not as a body of work within literature but as a tradition of political thought. She describes her book as "a study of and exercise in contemporary feminist utopian thought" (p 1) and her concern is to critique the notion of utopianism as 'perfection seeking' by examining the impact of feminist utopian thought in the theoretical works of feminist writers such as Monique Wittig (1992a, 1992b), Helene Cixous (1981) and Mary Daly (1980) and advocates the "transgressive utopian thinking" (p 4) these works exemplify.

Fictional and non-fictional feminist utopian writing produced since the beginning of second wave feminism with the emergence of the Women's Liberation Movement, is identifiable as a body of work in terms of their shared ideological standpoint and content as well as having a clear sense of audience. The line between fiction and non fictional feminist writing is blurred because, as well as shared themes there is a strong element of 'borrowing' between fiction and non-fiction in terms of genre: a number of fictional texts writers borrow from non-fictional genres such as an academic commentary at the close of Margaret Atwood's *The Handmaid's Tale* (1987). In non-fictional utopian writings such as *Ain't I a Woman* (1982) by bell hooks or Adrienne Rich's (1977) *Of Woman Born* there is the converse trend with problems and solutions being explored both through analytic writing and through myth, fiction and narratives of individual women's lives. It is this permeability of the boundary that adds to the significance of these works as a forum for debate within feminism.

A SPACE TO SPECULATE

Feminist utopian writing, both fictional and non-fictional, then offers the opportunity or 'space' to speculate, to imagine alternatives to the dominant order. There are difficulties, however, in viewing feminist utopias simply as spaces in which authentic femininity can be reclaimed or reconstructed. If we define a space as female, there is the danger of reifying traditional definitions of femininity which are generated from a position of subordination and marginalisation. Wolmark (1993), aware of these dangers of claiming that feminist science fiction utopias are a female space in which authentic female experience can be conceptualised, has suggested an alternative approach. She develops the concept of 'paraspace' which originated in relation to the fictional work of Samuel Delaney (1992) to map out the way in which these texts operate.

A 'paraspace' is a space that exists alongside and has a critical relationship with the dominant order but is not inscribed by the ideologies of this order. Instead, it is a space in which imaginative alternatives to the dominant order are experimented with. Conceptualising feminist utopian texts as a female space not only creates the danger of simply replicating traditional notions of femininity but further, it reinforces rather than challenges the founding ideas of patriarchy by maintaining a mutually exclusive two gender system. In the paraspace, instead, the founding ideas of patriarchy and its binary gender system can be challenged. This imaginative space is set alongside and outside the dominant order and "...is a space in which subjectivity and experience, gender and identity, can be re-imagined in opposition to, and in recognition of, the dominant gendered discourses" (Wolmark 1993, p 23). For feminist writers, utopias are narrative spaces in which the dominant patriarchal ideologies of gender can questioned and re-imagined. In a paraspace there is Showalter's (1986) 'double-voiced discourse', for, as Wolmark argues, this narrative space does not stand independently but has a "...contradictory relationship to the hegemonic discourses to which it is opposed but upon which it draws" (p 24) and is able to "...open up new spaces for alternative representations of gender..." (p 25). Characterising feminist utopian texts as 'paraspaces' emphasizes their dual role: existing alongside and acting both critically and imaginatively they can challenge the binary structures of masculine and feminine and offer alternative constructions of a gendered subjectivity.

Although Wolmark conceptualizes utopian writing as predominantly a fictional form, feminist utopianism is concerned with the process of conceptualisation and with attempts to transgress the dualist system of thinking about gender upon which patriarchal society is founded by the opening up of new conceptual spaces as part of an emancipatory project. Thus, for Sargisson utopian texts are the means through which feminists can engage in utopian thinking which she describes as:

> ... thinking that creates and operates inside a new place or space that has previously appeared inconceivable. Writing from or towards a good place that is no place, glancing over her shoulder at the place whence she came, the utopian feminist escapes restrictions of patriarchal scholarship. New and

> inventive languages can be imagined and employed in a new space, as can different social, sexual and symbolic relations (1996, p 41).

In feminist utopian texts, the future can be formed in an endless variety of ways, critically analysed and reformed. It is not predetermined but remains open to present action. By constructing future societies, feminist utopian writers not only critique the present patriarchal sociopolitical order but can reach, in the imagination, beyond the boundaries of patriarchy and pose alternative future possibilities both for a better society as well as for a transformed educative process.

SUMMARY

In summary, contemporary feminist utopian texts are not simply inventive narratives but are instead a diverse group of texts that are centrally concerned with the debate about the process of achieving a new social order. The sense of a 'willed-transformation' achieved through the actions of women has to be at the core of the text and, although the envisioned social order has 'Not-Yet-Become' it has in some ways to be a 'plausible' alternative, achievable through the agency of women. In these texts – both fictional and non fictional – the dilemmas, inconsistencies and gaps inevitable in any process of social transformation are exposed, examined critically and then compared to the issues and dilemmas facing women within contemporary society. The issue of gender is pivotal in these explorations of the idea of a better society. Education, too, is put under a critical lens from which alternative possibilities are generated. Feminist utopian thinking is the means to imagine 'the not-yet-conscious' ideas that we struggle to formulate as well as to formulate and interrogate ideas that are 'not-yet-become' around the question of gender and education. The 'not-yet-conscious' ideas potentially not only pose alternative forms of the educative process but hold out the possibility of ideas we have yet to conceive of let alone construct in policy and practice in relation to gender and education. It is in feminist utopian writings we see the development of alternative constructions of gender upon which we can develop policy and practice. And so, in the next chapter we discuss some early feminist utopian texts in order to explore the use of utopian thinking to debate the issue of women and education.

CHAPTER 3

EARLY FEMINIST UTOPIAN VISIONS

Introduction

Historically as part of women's claim of rights, education has been a significant element as this would empower women in challenging the structured inequalities within patriarchal society. It could seem that in a period when primary education, at least, is regard as a universal human right that women's campaigns for access to education are of only limited interest to debates about gender and educational futures. However, discussions of women's and girls' education in the early feminist utopian writings examined in this chapter help identify the questions we still grapple with today particularly in how we should conceptualise gender in educational policies and in practice. In this chapter I focus on some of the earliest 'feminist' writers who used the utopian genre to explore the education of girls and women in a period when education was not readily accessible even for girls and women of wealthy families.

As I argued in chapter two, the utopian genre includes both fictional and non-fictional forms, the defining feature of which is the construction of an alternative sociopolitical system no matter how tentative the proposal. In the texts examined here what we see are attempts to envisage a system or community in which women and girls could be educated. Clearly, there are issues in identifying specific texts written in an earlier historical period as 'feminist' given the twenty first-century understanding of the term. However, these texts explored take a knowing stance in relation to the position of women in society and the efforts to better this. Education is not seen as a personal issue concerned with solely the advancement of the individual, but the potential of women's education to be socially transformative is clearly recognised. The utopian genre, both fictional and non-fictional forms, enabled these writers to both critique the education of girls and women – such as it was – and debate the form this might take by constructing visions of alternative forms of education. In these texts questions are raised about both what should be included in women's education and where it should be conducted.

The texts discussed here were written over the period from the late seventeenth century to the late eighteenth century. Though it might be difficult to claim a tradition of specifically women's utopian writing with later texts being knowingly written in relation to earlier works, the writers discussed in this chapter were part of another broader tradition, that of 'the learned woman'. Gunther-Canada (2001) in her discussion of Wollstonecraft's transition from a female to a feminist reader places her work in an ongoing debate about women's education conducted through the publication of tracts and pamphlets over a lengthy period. By the late seventeenth century, there was a body of writing available by women for women and it is likely that the writers discussed here would be familiar with at least some of these texts which rehearse issues related to the position of women and education.

EARLY FEMINIST UTOPIAN WRITING

The most noteworthy of the books is Mary Wollstonecraft's (1988) *A Vindication of the Rights of Women* first published in 1792 which remains one of the seminal works on women's rights. In this text, where Wollstonecraft presents a cogent political analysis of the subordination of women, there is a strong visionary quality. Education is the means by which women would gain the necessary qualities to attain civil rights which would have a profound effect on the existing gender relations which were embedded in the sociopolitical structures. Wollstonecraft was contributing to a wider body of work. There are earlier examples of feminist utopian texts by Mary Astell, Clara Reeve and Sarah Scott in which, as Schnorrenberg (1982) argues each created an imaginary community of women where women could engage in educational and scholarly pursuits. These visions had a politically transformative purpose:

> Both Astell and Reeve were concerned primarily with the ideal communities for women to escape the worldly vanities, social pressures, and society's accepted concepts of what women's place ought to be. The goal was to establish a new atmosphere in which women could develop as individuals. Through their success in attracting and training their members, these communities could then spread out to reform society (p 266)

The principal utopian texts I will discuss in this chapter are Mary Astell's (1694) essay, *A Serious Proposal to the Ladies*, Sarah Scott's (1769) fictional utopia, *Millennium Hall* and Mary Wollstonecraft's *A Vindication of the Rights of Women* as they illustrate different treatments of the issue of gender and education. These texts were published before the idea that education is a universal human right and so discussions about women's education are very much concerned with access by girls and women from privileged sections of society. These authors each use the utopian genre to imagine alternative formations of education for women which would be socially transformative.

THE CHANGING POSITION OF WOMEN

The first of the utopian texts – Astell's *A Serious Proposal to the Ladies*– was written in the period following the Puritan Revolution in the mid seventeenth century in England. As the feminist historian Sheila Rowbotham (1974) notes, during the Puritan Revolution in the mid-seventeenth century, in sects such as the Shakers or Ranters the position of women underwent significant change: women took a more public and active role as men's equals and, in some instances, were leaders or prophetesses. Further, in these sects where belief centred on conscience and the individual's relationship with God, the spiritual equality of men and women was accepted. However, there was a gradual reversing of these trends and the Restoration period saw a retrenchment of a patriarchal gender hierarchy. At the same time, there were also changes in economic life which had an impact on the position of women. The Agricultural Revolution, the development of towns and the rise of, what Rowbotham terms, the 'middling classes' meant that the family was no longer a coherent economic unit in which all, both parents and children, contributed their labour to the family enterprise.

Debates about women's education in the late seventeenth century took place against a backdrop, and partly spurred on by, the changing position of women particularly the constraints imposed on women through marriage that reinforced patriarchal power structures. Women lost their autonomy and property on marriage. Marriage was the expected destiny of all girls; the options for those 'unfortunate' not to marry were extremely difficult especially if a woman had no financial support. Upper class marriage contracts could give some women personal freedom and could be mutually enriching and rewarding. However, such freedoms for women were dependent on the willingness of their husband to allow this and the structured inequalities in marriage between women and men were legally reinforced. Further, the domestic sphere came to be regarded as 'the proper space' for women particularly of those classes where there was sufficient income that women did not need to contribute monetarily. Following a dominant European trend since the Renaissance, an ideology underpinning women's domestic role evolved during the Restoration period and subsequently throughout the eighteenth century, in which a sentimentalised account of women was popularised culminating in the exaggerated form of femininity.

During this period there were numerous popular works through which dominant ideas about the position of women were circulated. There was also an outpouring of self-help material published in the genre of 'conduct books' (Todd, 1996) where discussions of the topics of marriage and education reinforced the dominant ideology of patriarchal gender relations. Conduct literature played an important role in the maintenance of patriarchal gender relationships to 'fit women for a contingent role' (Todd, 1996, p vii). As relatively few women could read, these books were written either for a male audience or to be read aloud by men to their families.

In the context of the excesses of the Restoration period, there was considerable concern about the conduct of women. The issue of female sexuality came under scrutiny and notions of female independence were rejected. As Todd argues "Fathers were frightened that learning would ruin what they regarded as the virtues of women: modesty, contentment and obedience" (p xi). It is in these works that attempts are made at an ideological level to shape female sexuality by sentimentalising women or exhorting them to Christian piety. Women's subordinate standing was further reinforced by the emergence of a medical discourse of sex difference based on biological differences. Women were positioned as being 'naturally' inferior to men both physically and psychologically. Consequently, any education a girl might receive should be about preparing them for their future domestic role and should not be intellectually too taxing. There would not only be social costs for a woman, making her too unattractive in men's eyes, but an extended or rigorous education might cause serious emotional damage. Thus a contemporary of Wollstonecraft's, Hester Chapone (1996) in *Letters on the Improvement of the Mind* argues against girls having a classical education in order to avoid becoming too severe, learned and, therefore, unattractive. Instead, Chapone exhorts women to be at all times modest and not to engage in flirtatious feminine behaviour.

There is a similar didactic stance in early feminist utopian works but where they differ from these other works is in the construction of alternatives to the status quo and thereby disrupting the conventional understandings underpinning the tracts, pamphlets and conduct books circulating at the time. Part of the strength of using the utopian genre is that women are able to imagine the possibility of alternatives being achieved through women's education. Though, as Schnorrenberg (1982) argues, the proposals in these works "...were not schemes for an entirely new world, but rather for the beginning of change, proposal to reform the present world" (p 270) and as such they enable us to consider the sociopolitical implications for women of different formations of education.

DISCUSSIONS ABOUT EDUCATION

In the seventeenth century a growing scholarly interest in the purposes and practices of education is reflected in Locke's work *Some Thoughts Concerning Education* (1690). Locke argued against innate qualities emphasizing instead the importance of the environment in early childhood and the need to draw out a child's qualities through careful formation. Education was as much a matter of development and formation of the individual as it was about acquiring skills and knowledge. Underlying the discussion about education was an unquestioned assumption that this was about the education of men/boys.

Education was largely through private tutors for boys of aristocratic families or grammar schools for boys of landed gentry. In the late seventeenth century, educational provision then began to expand not only in the number of schools but also in a widening of access with endowed schools for boys, and occasionally girls, of the poor which gave these children a rudimentary education. There was a growth in 'academies for daughters of gentlemen' (Charlton, 2002). Although this provision for girls continued to grow during the eighteenth century, the curriculum was very much related to the dominant ideologies of gender. Subjects that would enhance women's attractiveness were the core of the curriculum of these academies: music, dancing, writing, as well as French or another foreign language would be all part of a girl's accomplishments. Anticipating the girl's future domestic role, accounts were frequently included as one of the subjects. Latin, essential for access to further learning, if included, was rarely taught beyond the most rudimentary level.

The academies for the daughters of gentlemen were intended largely to prepare women for the marriage market and their role as wife and mother. For women education was equally limited as there were few opportunities for academic study and they had no access to university education. Following the dissolution of the abbeys during the Reformation in Britain, convents as both educative and religious communities were no longer available for women. Bathusa Makin (1980) in her essay *An Essay to Revive the Antient Education of Gentlewomen*, first published in 1673 looks back to this tradition "I verily think women were formerly educated in knowledge of arts and tongues and by their education many did rise to great heights in learning". In Britain there was no institutional access for women who wanted to engage in intellectual pursuits which stands in contrast to the educational opportunities afforded privileged women in continental Europe such as Anna Marie van Shurman, a scholar at the University of Utrecht whose work, *The Learned Maid* had been translated into English in 1659 (Hobby, 1988). Some women did engage in academic debates through their social networks most notably the 'Bluestockings' during the eighteenth century. The Bluestockings were a group of wealthy ladies and their friends who met together to engage in scholarly endeavours such as discussion, writing and sometimes publication. These networks also supported other women in their efforts to write and publish (Spender, 1986). It is against this background that early 'feminist' claims to education were made.

AN EDUCATIVE COMMUNITY

The idea of an institution dedicated to the intellectual development of women was something that engaged the imagination of a number of women writers over a long period. Margaret Cavendish, who in 1688 produced one of the first prose utopias by a woman, also wrote a number of plays set in alternative communities. In these plays Cavendish created exclusively female communities where women could withdraw in order to escape oppressive experiences of marriage. One play ends with a group of men from a rival male academy drowning out the women's discussions and although Bonin (2000) argues that this ending was intended to suggest that women cannot escape from the male dominance, I would argue that it also serves to illustrate the transgressive potential of the suggestion of a female educative community. An educational community for women was an attractive idea recurring in women's writings over the seventeenth and eighteenth centuries including works by Mary Astell and Sarah Scott.

Astell produced her utopian vision for a women's educational institution, *A Serious Proposal to the Ladies for the Advancement of their True and Greatest Interest*, in 1694. To a contemporary reader this proposal for a separate educational establishment may seem limited simply advocating women remove themselves from the possibility of mainstream education. However, as Perry (1986) reports, Astell's work "burst upon London in 1694 and was read and talked of from Pall Mall to Grub Street" (p 99). The text was reprinted four times within the first three years and the controversy it provoked prompted Astell to publish in 1697 *A Serious Proposal Part II* in which she engages in a sustained challenge to dominant assumptions about women's intellectual capabilities to support her case for the scholarly education of women within such an institution. A section of the text is guidance to her women readers to develop intellectual perseverance so they could enter into the theological and philosophical debates of the day.

In arguing for women's access to academic learning Astell rejects the dominant idea that women's primary concern must be marriage and that any limited education women and girls might access be solely concerned with the development of accomplishments to make a woman more marriageable. Unmarried women posed a particular challenge to patriarchal gender relationships which were institutionalised through marriage and so were very much marginalised, seen as 'unfortunate'. Astell, herself a single woman, claims a productive role for single women: "…the whole world is a single Lady's family" (p 150) and through being educated themselves, they could help form the next generation. Their chasteness affording them a purity of mind would carry more weight in challenging the vices of society than the arguments of the learned.

Astell also explicitly rejects Locke's claim that there is little point in teaching ethics or mathematics to day labourers or women by wittily posing a question of her women readers (to whom the proposal is directly addressed): "Can we Think and Argue Rationally about a Dress, an Intreague (sic), an Estate? Why then not upon better Subjects?" (p 111). There is no doubt Astell was proposing a place where women could engage in scholarly pursuits that would be demanding intellectually: the women in this retreat would "...busy themselves in a serious enquiry after *necessary* and *perfective* truths" (p 22, italics in the original).

In the customary education for girls, 'accomplishments' were more important that piety or intellectual understanding. Therefore in her proposal for a different kind of education, Astell has no place for literature, the learning of languages (unless necessary to access ideas) nor music. This is a sober place of purpose: "…no Impertinent Visits, no foolish Amours, no idle Amusements to distract our thoughts and waste our precious time" (p 29). Astell wanted to secure access to arenas that would satisfy her and other women of her class intellectually but otherwise her ambitions were limited. The proposal is addressed to ladies from aristocratic families or members of the landed gentry. Astell is also careful to allay concerns of any wider social and political change: "…women have no business with the Pulpit, the Bar or St Stephen's Chapel [that is, in the House of Commons]" (p 143). Instead women's role would be to improve society morally. We have to place Astell in her own period in a stratified society shaped by Christian doctrine and theological debates. She was, "a sincerely devout woman of high Anglican and Tory sympathies" (Hill 1986, p 2). Astell very much sets her discussion within a religious frame seeing a necessary relationship between knowledge and purity in order that women can make the right choice as defined by Christian doctrine. Education is then the means of protecting against temptations. In order to be a free agent and be responsible for their actions, women must have sufficient knowledge to make such reasoned choices:

> For the main thing we are to drive at in all our Studies, and that which is the greatest improvement of our Understandings is the Art of Prudence, the being all of a Piece, managing all our Words and Actions as it becomes Wise Persons and Good Christians (p 120).

Nevertheless in her argument for women's access to academic learning, Astell challenges the dominant ideology by refuting the viewpoint that women are not capable and are given over to 'folly'. She argues that "[t]he incapacity, if there be any, is acquired not natural; and none of their Follies are so necessary, but that they might avoid them if they be pleas'd themselves' (p 10) and ascribes them "to mistakes in our Education" (p 10). Women are first debarred from education and thereafter criticised for being absorbed by trivial matters.

The case for women accessing education, then, is made on religious grounds to ensure virtue and piety. It is on this basis, Astell puts forward her proposal for a 'monastery' or 'religious retirement' though withdrawal from the world is temporary. In this institution women would prepare to return to the world and engage in good works. It would be:

> ...a Seminary to stock the Kingdom with pious and prudent Ladies, whose good Example it is to be hop'd, will so influence the rest of their Sex, that Woman may no longer pass for those useless and impertinent Animals, which the ill conduct of too many has caus'd 'em to be mistaken for (p 21).

Although *A Serious Proposal Parts 1 and 11* stimulated great interest and criticism it did not lead to the idea of a women's educative community becoming a reality. One of the issues identified by Hill (1986) was the use of the term 'monastery' to describe this institution: in late 17th century Protestant England this term had overtones of Catholicism. However, it was not simply on the grounds of sectarian interests in religion that Astell's work posed a challenge but to the understanding of what it means to be a woman. Astell was criticized, on the one hand, because women were seen as being incapable of undertaking such a venture and on the other, for seeming to reject the dominant ideal of marriage being the rightful destiny of all women. As Springborg (1997) notes, there was a number of authors including Defoe who "expressing admiration for Astell's proposal argued against it on account of women's incorrigible levity" (p viii). In contrast, the essayist, Richard Steele writing in *The Tatler* describes Astell as "the founder of an 'order of Platonick Ladies" and criticizes her espousal of celibacy and her proposal that these women would "join their fortunes and erect a Nunnery" (cited by Springborg 1997, p xiii-xiv).

The ideas presented in these texts are concerned with re-defining what it means to be a woman in terms of intellectual capabilities in an era where "the learned lady" (Hill 1986, p 17) was the subject of satire. Astell's legitimises her claim to women's education on the basis of Christian ideals of piety and chastity. In other ways, Astell was clear in delineating the limits of her proposal and so this text may seem to be conserving of rather than challenging hierarchies of class. Education then was only for some women. Her proposal was for a retreat from the world for privileged women to equip them with the intellectual and religious strength to re-enter society and work to improve it morally. Underpinning this work is a construction of gender in which femininity is elided with piety, chastity and virtue. At one level, we can see this construction of what it means to be a woman as conservative, reinforcing patriarchal gender relationships. However, within this historical period, such a construction in which women could be seen as being capable of both intellectual pursuit and to some degree moral judgement, challenge the populist notions of an exaggerated femininity which was circulating at the time which centred on women's physical appearance and lack of ability.

The idea that through education, women – albeit privileged women – are able to contribute to the moral well being of society is a theme of the next utopia to be discussed, Sarah Scott'*s Millennium Hall* written in 1769 more than seventy years after Astell first published her work. Schorrenberg (1982) argues that, given that she was from a clerical and scholarly background, Scott most likely would have had access to Astell's *A Serious Proposal*. There are some strong resonances of Astell's proposal and the underpinning justification of *Millennium Hall.* Thus in *Millennium Hall,* the education of women has a higher religious and moral purpose but it is also seen as intrinsically fulfilling for the women involved. As Spender (1986) notes Scott's community of women "is certainly not seen as a consolation for women who have failed to marry" (p xiv). Though there are some strong similarities, there are also some interesting contrasts between what Astell proposed and Scott's vision of a suitable education for women.

A COMMUNITY OF WOMEN

Sarah Scott in her novel *Millennium Hall* was able to give a more expansive vision of an educational retreat for women. In the writings of Scott and Astell, we can see some of the debates about not only women's claim to education and also the type of education they should be able to access. Though both Astell and Scott propose a place separate from the world, the purpose of these communities and the educative process in which the women engage are subtly different. Both visions are very much set within Christian ideals but they differ in their treatment of what it means to be a woman.

Astell sought the legitimation of women's participation in intellectual pursuits and academic debate. Astell, therefore, places a strong emphasis on a scholarly education for these women. This is particularly evident in *A Serious Proposal Part II* where Astell guides her female readers in the practice of scholarly debate and writing. In Astell's proposal the women may return to the wider society as educators, either of their own children, or in the case of single women, other people's children, but this is, in some ways, a by-product an additional justification supporting her claim.

In contrast, Scott looks for a different form of education centring on what she sees are women's qualities. For Scott, the educative community becomes a separate social order founded on 'feminine' ideals which is a safe place for women. The novel is intended to persuade readers of this vision and uses the device typical of utopian fiction of travellers arriving for whom we have a detailed exposition of the purposes and structure of the community. The novel begins with a vision of the ideal educative community of Millennium Hall. This vision harks back to a 'golden age' both in the Arcadian setting of the Hall and in type of education conducted there. Though the main purpose of the community is one of nurturing the Christian ideals of piety and chastity, nevertheless women here can engage a form of the classical education that is denied them elsewhere. The reaction of one of the travellers is of awe:

> I could scarcely forbear believing myself in the Attic school. The room where they sat was about forty-five feet long, proportionable breadth, with three windows on one side, which looked into a garden, and a large bow at the upper end. Over against the windows were three large bookcases, upon the top of the middle one an orrery, and a globe on each of the others. In the bow sat two ladies reading with pen, ink and paper on the table before them at which was a young girl translating out of French. At the lower end of the room was a lady painting with exquisite art indeed, a beautiful Madonna; near her another, drawing a landscape out of her own imagination; a third, carving a picture-frame in wood, in the finest manner; a fourth engraving; and a young girl reading aloud to them; the distance from the ladies in the bow window being such that they could receive no disturbance from her. At the next window were placed a group of girls, from the age of ten years old to fourteen. Of these, one was drawing figures, another a landscape, a third a perspective view, a fourth engraving, a fifth carving, a sixth turning in wood, a seventh writing, an eighth cutting out linen, another making a gown, and by them an empty chair and a tent with embroidery, finely fancied, before it, in which we afterwards found had been left by a young girl who had gone to practice the harpsichord (p 7).

Education is both a haven for women as well as a means of developing their agency in making moral choices. Education enables them to grow in their understanding of Christian doctrine as well as providing opportunities to engage in Christian charity. One of the first places the visitors are taken is to see are the separate communities for socially marginalised groups. This utopia, however, is not a communitarian vision; there is a clear division between these groups and the ladies of the Hall. Thereafter, the purposes and benefits for women's education are explored through a number of narratives – 'the histories' of the women who founded Millennium Hall. Through these histories we are shown the consequences of an inadequate education particularly where women were vulnerable both economically and, in a libertarian milieu, to predatory male sexuality. The case for women's education is made through the juxtaposition of the women's past experiences and their lives at the Hall. As was noted earlier, the eighteenth century saw the establishment of 'academies for the daughters of gentlemen' providing the 'genteel education', the only type of education available for most upper and middle class women and girls. In the story of Lady Mary Jones we see results of this form of education in the frivolous conduct of Lady Sheerness who is the guardian of Lady Mary. Lady Sheerness leaves her charge open to the dangers of seduction:

> She had received a genteel education; no external accomplishments had been neglected; but her understanding and principles were left to the imperfection of nature corrupted by custom. Religion was thought too serious a thing for so young a person. The opinion of the world was represented to her as the true criterion by which to judge everything, and fashion supplied the place of every more material consideration (p 125).

And though Lady Sheerness was not naturally inclined to vice, because of her lack of education "...she became the victim of dissipation and the love of fashionable pleasures; destitute of any stable principles, she was carried full sail down the stream of folly" (p 126) which puts her charge Lady Mary in moral danger. It is only through the intervention of Miss Selvyn that Lady Mary is saved. As a result of her exceptional family circumstances, Miss Selvyn is a woman whose education in philosophy has been rigorous and so is able to guide Lady Mary to see the advances of her would-be seducer as improper rather than flattering. However though Miss Selvyn's education has been intellectually challenging through which she has developed a sober and scholarly mind, it, too, is lacking: her adoptive father had educated her well in academic subjects but, as someone who did not believe in the Christian faith, he had omitted any religious formation from Miss Selvyn's education. It is only in adulthood and through her protectress that Miss Selvyn realises a fuller education, one with Christian principles at its core.

It is this combination of intellectual development along with the nurturing of religious piety and virtue that is at the core of Scott's educational vision. Further, Scott regards education as a safe place for women – particularly vulnerable women without funds or family to support them. The opening history of Miss Mancel and Mrs Morgan (Miss Melvyn) follows them from their first meeting at an academy for daughters of gentlemen to their establishing Millennium Hall together. Their access to a wider education was partly by chance circumstance. Miss Melvyn had been banished to school by her stepmother and was kept there far longer than was usual. Miss Mancel's educational endeavours were supported by the indulgence of her guardian who, though, unbeknownst to the girl, was willing to provide any educational opportunity including a library of academic books, seeing this as part of the game of seduction which he hoped to conclude when Miss Mancel came of age.

> Nor was he sparing in what concerned her education, she learnt dancing, music and drawing; besides other things generally taught at schools; but her greatest improvement was from reading with Miss Melvyn, who instructed her in geography, and in such parts of philosophy someone of her age was capable of: but above all, she was most attentive to inculcate into her mind the principles of true religion (p 39-40).

It is only her association with Miss Melvyn that Miss Mancel has the ability to flee from her perilous circumstance and find an alternative life. Millennium Hall then is presented as the living realisation of Christian virtues of piety, chastity and charity but it is clearly also a place, which is vibrant and fulfilling for the women who live there.

Kelly (1999) argues that Scott's novel *Millennium Hall* is "the manifesto of bluestocking feminism, itself a major attempt to re-define class and gender relations at a critical point in the transformation of English society and culture" (p 43). The term 'manifesto' imbues the author with a knowing political positioning. Scott was indeed well connected with this group of intellectual women, being the sister of Lady Elizabeth Montagu, one of the leading figures in the Bluestockings circle. As a utopian novel, *Millennium Hall* provides a critique of the existing situation with regard to women's education side by side with a vision of a possible alternative for women's education. Further, the purpose of the text is social transformation in ways not suggested by Astell's proposal. Access to learning and other cultural pursuits, though important, are to come second to these aspirations. This partly explains why, in contrast to Astell's proposal, in Scott's utopian community as an expression of their Christian piety and charity there is an active concern for marginalized groups. The education of children of the poor, however, reinforces rather than challenges social hierarchies: the girls are educated to prepare them for work in service or for their role as a farmer's wife. And boys are educated on the estate to prepare them for their work as labourers.

Both Astell and Scott envisaged women's education as separate from that of men. However, the debate evolved in the course of the nineteenth century. Todd (1989) indicates that the arguments in the mid-eighteenth century in relation to how much learning women should have access gave way to a "discussion of the gendered intellect and whether or not there are masculine and feminine areas of intellectual life" (p 211). In educational terms this was translated into an argument about whether there was a gendered educational process pointing to the need for a different form of education for women and girls or whether they should have the right to receive the same classical form of education as was available to their brothers. We can see this debate being conducted in the 1790s through the writings of, among others, Catherine Macaulay and Mary Wollstonecraft.

THOUGHTS ON THE EDUCATION OF DAUGHTERS

Mary Wollstonecraft is often seen as producing the first major work on women's rights in which the education of women is an important foundation. Mary Wollstonecraft's own experiences were formative. She was able to access only limited education and had to pursue scholarly learning through her own endeavours. She also was a teacher, running a school with her sisters and for a while, a governess. Though neither of these experiences were particularly fulfilling for Wollstonecraft they helped shape her thinking in her first work *Thoughts on the Education of Daughters* published in 1787 (Todd, 2004).

Richardson (2002) argues that education is a theme running through much of Wollstonecraft's writings. The first work *Thoughts on the Education of Daughters* reads very much like "the work of a young author wishing to appeal to mainstream tastes by reiteration received ideas…" (Richardson 2002, p 26). *Thoughts on the Education of Daughters* was written in the tradition of 'conduct books' – advice literature – and in many aspects she draws on conventional understandings of the development and education of girls. This book deals with those areas commonly covered in such works: early child rearing in the nursery, dress and external accomplishments. There is the strong moralistic tone of advice literature: "...children are taught revenge and lies in their very cradle" (p 9) and advice is given about how best to avoid these circumstances.

Although there is much conventional advice offered in this first book, there are the beginnings of her argument about the development of rational beings.

Wollstonecraft advocated the education of the young: "[i]ntellectual improvements like the growth and formation of the body, must be gradual – yet there is no reason why the mind should lie fallow" (p 17). The threads are there also in Wollstonecraft's criticism of the fashionable type of affected femininity. She dismisses being the "genteely educated" (p 77, italics in the original) and highlights the "unfortunate situation of females, fashionably educated and, left without a fortune" (p 69) who were debarred from an education that would make them financially independent. The roles of teacher, companion and governess were the only roles open for women who had no financial resources but, from her own experiences, these roles from Wollstonecraft's own experiences, were not necessarily fulfilling.

EDUCATION AND RIGHTS

Though some of the seeds of Wollstonecraft's major work on education are to be found in this earlier book, there is a significant development in her ideas between the first book and *A Vindication of the Rights of Women.* She draws from her involvement in debates about rights against the backdrop of the French Revolution – she had previously published *A Vindication of the Rights of Man* in 1790 – and from her reading of contemporaneous works on the subject of female education. She wrote a number of reviews of works on this subject for the *Analytical Review* (Todd and Butler, 1989) including in 1790 a review of Catherine Macaulay's *Letters on Education* (1996). Wollstonecraft drew from these discussions to develop a coherent and closely argued case for the education of women and girls on the same terms as their brothers.

In her letters about the educational process, Macaulay made only intermittent reference to the issue of gender. The most focussed discussion of gender is in *Letter XXII: No Characteristic Difference in Sex.* She contends that the difference in character and behaviour of the sexes in social contexts has been used to argue that there are differences in terms of intellect based on gender: "...much false speculation on the natural qualities of the female mind" (Macaulay 1996, p 203). She takes issue with Rousseau's contention of the existence of innate sex differences arguing instead that the superior physical strength of men, which previously was vital to survival, has long after been used to perpetuate the inequalities between the sexes: it has been used "...to destroy all natural rights of the female species, and reduce them to a state of abject slavery" (p 206). She sees this being perpetuated by the only education available to women: "the situation and education of women, Hortensia [to whom the letters are addressed] is precisely that which must necessarily corrupt and debilitate both the powers of the mind and body (p 207). Not only are girls taught to be overly conscious of their physical appearance from an early age, but their moral education is lacking "...everything that ennobles our being, and that renders us innoxious and useless, is either taught, or mistaught in such a manner as to leave us no proper impression on the mind" (p 208). Instead, the purpose of the education of girls is to make her "agreeable to her husband" (p 209).

In her review of Macaulay's book Wollstonecraft (1989) highlights several points that she then pursues in her own work: in the education of children at home "the amusements and instruction of boys and girls should be the same" (p 311) as should also be the reading material they are each given. Most importantly, Wollstonecraft agrees with Macaulay's views on women's education refusing to entertain the various objections put forward repeatedly and instead proclaiming that, like Macaulay, she knows "...of no learning, worth having, that does not tend to free the mind from error, and enlarge our stock of useful knowledge" (p 314). In her discussion of the specific letter that deals with gender, Wollstonecraft wishes that the argument could have gone further, an idea she then takes into her own study.

Wollstonecraft is forthright in her criticism of the education women had access to: "the neglected education of my fellow-creatures is the grand source of the misery I deplore" (p 7). It is a "false system of education" (p 7). She is also concerned to critique previous commentaries on women's education: "all writers who have written on the subject of female education and manners from Rousseau to Dr Gregory, have contributed to render women more artificial, weak characters, than they otherwise would have been." (p 22).

Wollstonecraft was opposed to the traditional form of education open to women in which the purpose of education has been limited to developing some "corporeal accomplishment" (p 23) to render women pleasing. The current state of women's education is "disorderly" in which the "cultivation of understanding is always subordinate" (p 23). This Wollstonecraft sees as robbing women of their abilities and resulted in behaviours and attitudes that perpetuate their place as subordinate and irrational creatures incapable of education. She examines in detail both the psychological and social impact of the current approach to the education of women.

> Novels, music, poetry, and gallantry, all tend to make women the creatures of sensation, and their character is thus formed in the mould of folly during the time they are acquiring accomplishments, the only improvement they are excited, by station in society, to acquire. This over stretched sensibility naturally relaxes other powers of the mind, and prevents intellect from attaining that sovereignty which it ought to attain to render a rational creature useful to others, and content with its own station: for the exercise of the understanding, as life advances, is the only method pointed out by nature to calm the passions (p 61).

Wollstonecraft argues against "careful education" where women are domesticated to become drudges. Instead, she intends to treat women "like rational creatures" (p 9) and so "every being may become virtuous by exercise of their own reason" (p 21). She argues for a more rigorous education where "reason is absolutely necessary to enable a woman to perform any duty properly, and I must repeat, that sensibility is not reason" (p 64). Wollstonecraft maps out the positive aspects of women being educated which would lead to significant changes "even love would acquire more serious dignity" (p 119). She argues that:

> The most perfect education, in my opinion, is such an exercise of the understanding as is best calculated to strengthen the body and form the heart.

> Or, in other words, to enable the individual to attain such habits of virtue as will render it independent. (p 21).

Where Wollstonecraft differs from Astell and Scott is in her forthright rejection of the construction of a separate sphere for women including education. There is a sharp contrast between Astell's proposal for a monastery or 'religious retreat', Scott's *Millennium Hall* and Wollstonecraft's rejection of any suggestion of separate provision, of "being shut away" (p 128). Wollstonecraft counters the many claims put forward that the attaining of virtue is very different for women and men by taking Rousseau's position and applying this to women, arguing that "every being may become virtuous by the exercise of their own reason" (p 21) – both women and men have souls and so they should be seeking the same thing. Part of Wollstonecraft's objection to separation is that women are too intimate which simply reinforces frivolity rather than nurtures the development of rigorous thought.

> I object to many females being shut together in nurseries, schools, or convents. I cannot recollect without indignation, the jokes and hoiden [sic] tricks, which knots of young women indulge themselves in, when in my youth accident threw me, an awkward rustic, in their way. They were almost on a par with the double meanings, which shake the convivial table when the glass has circulated freely (p 128).

Instead Wollstonecraft argues for boys and girls to have access to the same education indicating that any differences between boys and girls are not the result of innate difference but are the result of contrasting educational experiences. Wollstonecraft claims that where there is a similar educational experience, there is no difference between the sexes. Wollstonecraft takes up from Macaulay's exposition on sex difference:

> I will allow that bodily strength seems to give a man a natural superiority over woman; and this is the only solid basis on which the superiority of the sex can be built. But I still insist, that not only the virtue but the *knowledge* of the sexes should be the same in nature, if not in degree, and that women, considered not only as moral, but rational creatures, ought to endeavour to acquire human virtues (or perfections) by the *same* means as men, instead of being educated like a fanciful kind of *half* being" (p 39, italics in the original).

Part of Wollstonecraft's utopian vision is the establishment of a national education system. She sets out her plan for education outlining structures for the staffing of such schools and for pupil discipline and the curriculum. Wollstonecraft also concerns herself with the curriculum declaring that there should be limits to sedentary employment with practical subjects particularly gymnastics playing an important part. Further, these day schools would be part of a national system in which there are paid teachers. The professionalisation of teachers would ensure that the task of teaching is one of developing the intellect rather than the superficial pleasing of the parents (on whom teachers in England at the time had to rely on to be paid).

Central in this plan is co-education with boys and girls learning together and mixing freely from which there are significant intellectual benefits to be gained even in childhood:

> Girls and boys, in short, would play harmlessly together, if the distinction of sex was not inculcated long before nature makes any difference. – I will go further, and affirm, as an indisputable fact, that most of the women, in the circle of my observation, who have acted like rational creatures, or shown any vigour of intellect, have accidentally been allowed to run wild – as some of the elegant formers of the fair sex would insinuate (p 43).

In this formation of education lie the seeds of social and political change. However, it is not just about mixing with the opposite gender but also mixing with one's own peer groups. Here, unlike the respect demanded in exchanges with parents and other adults, there is equality and so children learn independence and the ability to put forward their viewpoint. These experiences create the questioning mind that Wollstonecraft sees as fundamental to any claim of rights. Wollstonecraft is arguing for women's access to the same form of classical education that is available to their male peers. Access to this form of education is the foundation upon which women can seek political change. By being educated in this way, women could develop the rational capabilities necessary for them to base their claim of rights.

CHALLENGES FOR EDUCATION TODAY

These early visions of an educational future are important because we can see how the construction of education is shaped on different understandings of gender. During the period covered by these works, the construction of 'femininity' was as complex and at times contradictory as it is today. As England dealt with massive social and economic changes in the last decade of the eighteenth century "women were increasingly assigned to the central role of maintaining 'moral institutions''' (Poovey 1984, p 9) particularly the family. In this sociopolitical context, the dominant ideology of what it means to be a woman was complex: 'female' and 'feminine' became conflated leading to the paradox that femininity is both innate and needs to be reproduced through acculturation. Though the ideal of a moral superiority was reproduced through a range of pamphlets, periodicals and novels, at the same time there was an underpinning assumption that women's appetites must be controlled; chastity was essential. Where sexuality was sublimated in woman's vanity and their need for praise, women were exhorted to be modest at all times and not to seek the public domain: "...women were encouraged to display no vanity, no passion, no assertive self at all (Poovey 1984, p 21). However, this did not go unchallenged.

These early feminist utopian writings challenged the conventional ideas about what it meant to be a woman. Common across all these works is the critique of the dominant ideology of the time, particularly the exaggerated form of femininity defined in terms of appearance, manners and flirtatious behaviour. Rejection of this ideal femininity was based on proposing alternative constructions of what it means to be female which could be achieved through an improved educational process for women. Arguing for a life of the mind, as each of these authors did, was a radical position to adopt. Women supported their claim to education by arguing that this would be the means of nurturing Christian ideals of piety and chastity but these had to be based on rational thought. For these writers, the dominant ideologies of gender limited women's personal development for Astell as a scholar, for Scott as an independent woman and for Wollstonecraft as citizen. Though there are similarities there are also some significant differences between the three visions of education.

One of the contrasts is women's role in the public domain. Both Astell and Wollstonecraft argue for women to gain entry into scholarly education, an education fitting them to engage in the critical debates of their day. For Astell, though the purpose behind this was to enable women to prepare for Christian redemption. For Wollstonecraft the purpose is to develop an active role in social and political life. In contrast, Scott sees women creating a separate – and better – society. These differences in the purpose reflect contrasting understandings of what it means to be a woman and the sociopolitical implications of this construction. Stafford (2002) highlights how Hannah More, who opposed Wollstonecraft's proposal, nevertheless advocated for women to study geography, natural history logic and philosophy. However, the purpose behind this education is to enable women's minds to be strengthened so they would not be vulnerable to temptation and seduction (Stafford, 2002).

SUMMARY

These early visions may seem distant from contemporary concerns particularly in their handling of class issues. While Astell very much confines her vision to a select group of privileged women, Scott sees that a rudimentary education at least should be available to the children of the poor though this was gendered and class based, being very much geared towards their future occupational and domestic roles. It is Wollstonecraft's who anticipates a national system open to all that we, perhaps, are more comfortable with in terms of contemporary orthodoxies. However, an exploration of these three early utopian texts by women has helped not only to plot the development of the debate about women's education historically but also underline the potential of feminist utopian thinking to inform discussions about educational futures and gender. As women historically have been excluded systematically from full access to education on the basis of their gender, inevitably the focus in these early visions is principally on female education.

There is a tendency in current debates about gender, to locate advocacy for educational opportunities for women and girls narrowly within the efforts of the radical feminism of the 1970s. The progress women have made in education is seen as aberrational and now the balance which was disturbed by the doctrinaire claims of a minority of radical women, needs to be redressed. To set these debates about gender in a longer historical frame illustrates that the question of gender in education has been a significant issue for far longer and so we can resist the simplistic reasoning that pits the claims for education by women/girls against the needs of men/boys. These early debates about women's education illuminate some of the challenges we currently face in looking to achieve the position of universal access to education by women and girls globally. However, these discussions have implications not just for women's education but the treatment of the broader question of gender in educational policy and practice. Answers to why and how we educate women and girls, men and boys rest on how we construct gender. In the next chapter I discuss ideologies of gender.

CHAPTER 4

IDEOLOGIES OF GENDER

Introduction

In the previous chapter we saw how early feminist utopian writers challenge the dominant ideologies of femininity by providing different visions what it means to be a woman. For Astell this vision was of women as scholars, for Scott, women as social conscious agents, for Wollstonecraft, women as citizens. These different visions illustrate that what it means to be a woman is not a simple unchanging idea but is a dynamic concept, the meaning of which is contested. The debates about what it means to be 'a woman' are various: is, for example, the concept of 'woman' a social construct or is derived from a set of essential qualities whether biological or psychological or even, whether the concept of 'being a woman' is a useful notion on which to base political action. This debate raises questions not just about how we deal with gender in education of girls and women, boys and men but also questions whether we should be even using the construct of gender as a basis for shaping educational policy and practice. In this chapter I examine different ideological constructions of gender found in feminist utopian writing. The purpose of this book is to explore feminist utopian writings and consider critically the implications for policy and practice in relation to gender and education.

Julia Kristeva's essay *Women's Time* (1991), in which she explores the development of feminist thought and politics, is especially pertinent to a discussion about gender and education within feminist utopian thinking because it is itself an example of a feminist non-fictional utopian work. Kristeva examines the relationship in feminist thought between the process of social change and the conception of what it means to be a woman by identifying three phases: (1) the struggle for equal rights (2) the development of woman-centred approaches (3) the creation of a sociopolitical order where gender is no longer significant.

In this chapter I will, firstly, consider whether Kristeva's hypothesis of three phases or positions within feminist thought can be used productively in relation to discussions about the educative process in feminist utopian writing. It is also important to remember that debates about what it means to be a woman within feminism are set against the backdrop of patriarchal ideologies of masculinity and femininity. As a preliminary, therefore, I will consider, patriarchal ideologies of femininity and masculinity before moving on to explore in detail each of the three broad positions identified by Kristeva and then consider their use as a framework to examine the discussions about gender and the educative process in feminist utopian writing. The examination of each of these three positions will draw on material from a range of theorists representative of particular positions. It is important to indicate that the intention at this point is not to advocate for a specific position or argument proposed by any one theorist but instead to outline the underpinning ideas of each phase, because it is from these discussions that feminist utopian writers draw their ideas in the construction of the good society.

KRISTEVA'S THREE PHASES OF FEMINISM

The first and second phases, the struggle for equal rights and the development of woman-centred approaches were evident when Kristeva wrote her essay in 1979 but the third phase was just beginning to be developed. In this third phase the founding idea of the preceding phases, that is, the notion of 'woman' as the basis of a radical politics, is questioned: "...the very dichotomy man/woman as an opposition between two rival entities may be understood as belonging to *metaphysics*" (p 458, italics in the original).

Kristeva begins the essay *Women's Time* by arguing that considerable attention has been focussed on the issue of space in relation to gender but little has been considered in relation to time. Kristeva proposes that feminism can be viewed profitably in terms of 'generations'; feminist thought is dynamic, with ideas evolving and being debated over long periods. These phases, though, can only to some extent be placed chronologically: the emergence of the Women's Liberation Movement (WLM) around 1968 is cited as the divide between the first and second phases and the third phase is said to begin emerging in the mid-1980s. It is more productive to view each 'phase' as a "...signifying space..." (p 458) with all three phases able to co-exist as competing positions within contemporary feminism. As we saw in the previous chapter early women writers adopted different positions with Wollstonecraft claiming equality with men while Scott suggests an alternative woman-centred community. Viewing each approach as a concurrent ideological position rather than a specific historical phase fits Kristeva's focus in this essay. The first phase, the demand for equal rights, and the second phase, the development of woman-centred approaches have been concurrent positions throughout the development of feminism. These phases mark a continuing debate with one or the other more dominant at a particular period while the possibility of a third position Kristeva suggests was only beginning to be conceived at the time she wrote *Women's Time* in the late 1970s and is now articulated in the theoretical works of writers such as Judith Butler (1990, 1993).

In Kristeva's first phase, women, by claiming equal rights, are rejecting the limiting effects of becoming a woman: of becoming 'feminine'. The different behaviours and characteristics of women and men, evident in patriarchal society, are seen as the result of differential patterns of socialisation that place women in subordinate roles. Women are socialised to become 'feminine', that is, acquire those characteristics such as nurturance and passivity which lead women to being placed in powerless positions. The task, therefore, is to reject any notions of femininity, these being inherently oppressive. In contrast, in the second phase, 'being a woman' is reclaimed as a positive role; being a woman means to have as part of your identity a set of essential qualities, which differ from the qualities men possess. By virtue of biological makeup or through their social experiences, women come to possess vital qualities such as connectedness and nurturance that should be reclaimed as valuable. The major difference between these first two phases is the treatment of femininity and masculinity; whereas in the first phase femininity and masculinity are seen to be qualities that can be displayed by both men and women, in the second phase, femininity and masculinity are seen as mutually exclusive sets of qualities with femininity now constituting the valued set of qualities.

Kristeva rejects both the demand for equality and the woman-centred approaches viewing each as fundamentally flawed. She questions the concept of 'woman' as a viable foundation in the struggle for social change because it maintains the idea that the differences between women and men should have a sociopolitical outcome, a proposition so far which has only worked to the detriment of women by perpetuating their subordination. Consequently, she advocates the third position or attitude that is beginning to be formulated. It is in the discussion of the third phase that we can see clearly the utopian focus of Kristeva's essay: "this third attitude, which I strongly advocate – which I imagine?" (p 458). In this essay there is a speculative and imaginative formulation of ideas that, at present, do not have a material reality. Kristeva argues that we should abandon the concept of 'woman' because it is a construct defined by the symbolic order of patriarchy. However, what specifically we should replace this construct with is only being explored in speculative and creative works.

> It seems to me that the role of what is usually called 'aesthetic practices' must increase... to demystify therefore the community of language as a universal and unifying tool, one which totalizes and equalizes (p 457).

This third phase has emerged particularly in two areas, high theoretical writings that draw from post modernism, in which writers interrogate and destabilize the concept of gender and in feminist science fiction utopias notably cybertopias. The question remains whether it is possible to make concrete the sociopolitical consequences of this position. Kristeva argues that we must consider "...along with the singularity of each person...the multiplicity of every person's identifications" (p 459) and this seems to suggest not simply that definitions of what it means to be a woman are varied but more fundamentally it raises the problem of whether any definition is possible or even desirable. In the remainder of this chapter I discuss patriarchal ideologies of gender before moving on to examine these competing definitions of what it means to be a woman in feminist thinking and politics.

PATRIARCHAL IDEOLOGIES OF FEMININITY AND MASCULINITY

Within patriarchy, the concepts of gender and sex have a political significance determining especially the distribution of power between women and men. However, the material workings of these concepts are far from visible because, within the traditional ideologies of femininity and masculinity, the differential positions of women and men in patriarchy are held to be 'natural'. The concepts of 'feminine' and 'female' are elided, as are the concepts of 'masculine' and 'male'. As a result, the biological traits of women and men are regarded as the source of all perceived differences including those of personality, social behaviour and intellectual capabilities. The concepts of female/feminine and male/masculine, held as universal, natural and exclusive, are used to structure the inequitable distribution of power. The categories of femininity and masculinity are constructed as mutually exclusive with masculinity as the positive pole because the 'masculine' attributes of strength, competitiveness and aggression are valued within patriarchal society, whereas women's 'true nature', their perceived lack of strength and aggression, places them in the less powerful position and their tasks are the less valued ones of nurturing and caring within the private domain of the family.

The relative positions of men and women within society are maintained through the structures of the patriarchal family and women's role within the family shapes perceptions, not only of their social capabilities but also of their psychological development towards true femininity. In patriarchal ideologies 'women's nature' – our femininity – is defined primarily by our childbearing and sexual function. This construction of women's nature is illustrated graphically in Freud's (1977a, 1977b) theory of psychosexual development. Freud drew from the prevailing cultural attitudes with regard to women in Western Europe to explain psychosexual development. In Freud's explanation, femininity and masculinity are structured by 'normal' heterosexuality, an important feature of which is the distinction between the active male role and the passive female role. This is not an equal division, because maleness/masculinity remains not only the valued dimension but is regarded as the normative, 'human' experience and indeed, for a period of time the girl will assume a masculine character in terms of her emotional and sexual development in early childhood; she is made 'different' through a traumatic psychic event. The event that sends her on the route to true femininity – from activity to passivity in both her social and sexual behaviour – is her discovery of a biological 'deficiency', her lack of a penis. The resulting psychosexual structures become the determinants of normal femininity: the recognition of the lack of a penis is used to explain characteristics such as passivity, narcissism and shame which are the features of femininity that 'real women' should display. The course of psychosexual development is not inevitable in a determinist sense; there are alternative responses that the young girl can make: sexual frigidity or reversion to masculinity, that is homosexuality, but these are not the 'normal' responses. The normal response within Freud's paradigm is in fact to enter into a heterosexual relationship in which women are subordinate.

Within heteropatriarchy the primacy of male heterosexuality has repercussions for the social status and rights of women. Partly arising out of Judeo-Christian traditions, a moral code of behaviour underpinning 'true femininity' is defined in terms of maternity, passivity and purity; 'normal' women can only be wives and mothers or virgins, the latter being a particularly powerless position because a virgin cannot acquire the status that accrues to a woman by virtue of her relationship with a man. Women who refuse these functions and instead assume autonomous roles, the lesbian or 'Amazon' of myth, are not 'natural'; these women can only be either 'bad or mad' because, to deviate from the code, is to be not only unfeminine but also to be abnormal. By limiting the roles open to us, the structure of the patriarchal family has a profound effect on the material position of women determining not only what roles we are able to play but also what roles we ought to fulfil. It also shapes our lives at an ideological level. Okin (1980) suggests that the questions raised in patriarchal political thought have tended to focus on the nature of 'man', the purpose of which has been to distinguish between innate potential and the effects of socialisation. In contrast, there has long been a tendency to define women in terms of the function they serve for men. A text that has been highly influential on progressive education, Rousseau's *Emile* (1993) is an obvious example. In this text, Emile's abilities are examined when he is free from the limiting effects of society but Sophie is presented not as an autonomous individual but simply in relation to his needs. She has no agency and her learning concerns only her subordinate role. In Simone De Beauvoir's (1977) terms: "He is the subject, he is absolute – she is the Other" (p 16).

Susan Brownmiller in her study, *Femininity* (1984), points to the ongoing strength of patriarchal definitions of femininity in determining the status of women and in the value individual women are assumed to place upon themselves in patriarchal society:

> To be insufficiently feminine is viewed as a failure in core sexual identity, or as a failure to care sufficiently about oneself, for a woman found wanting will be appraised (or will appraise herself) as mannish or neutered or simply unattractive, or as men have defined these terms (p 15).

Brownmiller's statement reflects the consequences for women of the traditional ideologies of femininity. Women's position as subordinate is further intensified by the construct of the ideal or essential woman. The specific determinants of the ideal woman may vary according to the current fashion, but as De Beauvoir (1972) argues, the fact that there is a notion of the ideal woman will exclude and oppress numerous women and will also deny significant differences between women.

Feminist utopian writers have extrapolated from contemporary societal trends to reveal the oppression of women. In non fictional utopian writings, for example, *Gyn/Ecology* (1984) by Mary Daly or 'Our Blood: The Slavery of Women in Amerika' (sic) (1982) by Andrea Dworkin, contemporary society dominated by patriarchal ideologies is the dystopia and the violence, both physical and psychological, against women are depicted as being endemic. In *Gyn/Ecology* Daly presents a grim picture of both traditional cultural practices such as footbinding, suttee and genital mutilation and what she conceives of as equivalent practices in industrialized western societies, for example, cosmetic surgery or the medicalisation of normal changes in women's lives such as menopause.

Patriarchal ideologies form the basis of the dystopian societies against which feminist eutopian alternatives are formed. A characteristic feature of feminist utopian fiction is the interaction between eutopian and dystopian constructs of alternative societies within a specific text or across a number of texts. There are strong resonances between the images presented in the non-fictional works of writers like Daly and Dworkin and the construction of dystopian societies in fiction. In fictional utopias, such as *A Walk to the End of the World* (1989) by Suzy

McKee Charnas, the oppression of women within patriarchal society is similarly graphically depicted. Women in dystopias are there merely to serve the needs of men, whether this is as an enslaved labour force, or as the bearers of the next generation of men or as sexual slaves and victims of male violence.

In Charnas's text, in the extreme society of Holdfast there is no thought to educate women: they are there simply to reproduce the next generation of men. These dystopian images might seem distant from the context of educational systems particularly within western democracies. However, in feminist utopian writing, by taking the patriarchal constructs of femininity and masculinity to their logical extreme, feminist writers depict the profound effects that ideologies have on both the psychological and material experiences of women. These texts point to the deep sense of alienation women experience within male-inscribed forms of education which privilege masculine qualities such as competitiveness and adversarial forms of debate that relegate women to the sidelines. Further, what is regarded as appropriate education for women is defined in terms of their reproductive and domestic roles. This shapes not only what women/girls learn but also their access to different areas of education, particularly higher education.

THE CLAIM FOR EQUAL RIGHTS

In patriarchal regimes women are circumscribed by their domestic roles as wife and mother and a distinction is made between the private sphere, the domestic world of home and family, which is regarded as the rightful place of women, and the public world of men. Therefore, patriarchal definitions of femininity need to be modified to encompass a wider range of behaviours and attributes. One response to patriarchal ideas about what it means to be a woman is to claim that a woman is fundamentally the same as a man and, therefore, women should be treated as equals to men and have the same rights. As was argued in the previous chapter, the claim for equal rights has a long history in feminism in which of particular note is Mary Wollstonecraft's *A Vindication of the Rights of Woman* published in 1792. This position – the claim for equality – is evident in feminist utopian writing by women of previous generations when particularly middle class women sought access to areas that were traditionally deemed suitable only for men particularly higher education, work and politics. Feminist utopias produced during first wave feminism such as Florence Dixie's (1890) *Gloriana or the Revolution of 1900* play out these debates. Here Dixie presents a vision of a new and better society led by a woman.

In these early discussions about women's rights no clear distinction is made between sex and gender, but in the more recent equal rights debate of the 1960s and 1970s, this crucial distinction is made, with the term 'sex' referring to the biological attributes of femaleness and maleness and the term 'gender' referring to those features of human behaviour that are distinguished within cultural norms as feminine and masculine. The separation of these concepts has been a vital step in the development of feminist theory and politics because the distinction made between sex and gender has enabled feminist theorists to reveal the profound and deleterious influence of a culture underpinned by patriarchal ideologies on women's lives. As De Beauvoir (1977) demonstrates, the mythical patriarchal construct of the 'eternal feminine' is used to position women in a subordinate social position. The potency of this construct is clearly visible when women's lives and experiences run counter to this ideal: when there is this clash between ideal and experience, it is not the ideal that is judged to be flawed but instead it is the women who fail to meet this ideal who are flawed: they are simply not feminine enough. The distinguishing between the physical features of femaleness and maleness (sex) from the set of cultural practices and attitudes (gender) was an important step because it allowed feminists to highlight male dominance as a critical aspect in the oppression of women, arguing that gender inequality was not simply the inevitable result of biological differences.

Important also is the idea that 'femininity' and 'masculinity' are attributes found to differing degrees in both women and men. The concept of 'androgyny' as the merging of femininity and masculinity then can challenge the patriarchal notion of a gendered nature and form the basis of a new social order. There are a number of examples of feminist utopias based on this position from earlier periods. *Unveiling A Parallel* (1991) by Alice Ilgenfritz Jones and Ella Merchant (published in 1893) is a good example in which the authors compare nineteenth century American society to a future society in which women enjoy the same kind of privileges, especially with regard to the sexual double standard enjoyed by men. However, this alternative society is constructed simply to demonstrate the limitations of traditional understandings of masculinity and women's emulation of this. The eutopian or good society is the third one visited in which the inhabitants have been able to create a better society by merging the best qualities in relation to the characteristics displayed by women and men within patriarchal society.

Within second wave feminism there was a revisiting the concept of 'androgyny', the merging of masculine and feminine qualities. Carolyn Heilbrun (1973), among others, suggests that a gendered perception of human nature should be replaced by the idea of androgyny. In Heilbrun's view, androgyny results from a merging of femininity and masculinity which would dispense with the need for gender roles to be rigidly endorsed and policed by traditional notions of appropriateness. Instead, the individual would be free to choose her or his own mode of behaviour. If these patterns of behaviour can be changed, then the social structures which rest upon these notions of femininity and masculinity such as the divide between public and private spheres or the roles within the family can also be altered. However, the idea of androgyny has not afforded a redistribution of power and though there is an attractive ideal underpinning this notion, ultimately because of its location within an equal rights discourse, androgyny has become associated with the masculinisation of women. Consequently, the position of masculinity as the positive pole remains unchallenged and so the discussions in feminism about the distinctive and valuable attributes of being a woman came to the fore.

As Kristeva notes in her essay, the argument for equal rights has not led to the widespread liberation of women. The claim for equal rights has resulted in material benefits for women particularly in developed economies including access to education but globally a significant numbers of women do not engage in and may even be actively excluded from formal education. A new social order has not emerged and the claim for equal rights has brought about no radical change for the majority of women including removing the limitations on the educational opportunities of significant numbers of women, largely because the values underpinning patriarchy are not challenged sufficiently. Critics of this position, including Kristeva, argue that the claim for equal rights centres on demonstrating women's capabilities within traditional male spheres; women are expected to assume the behaviours, aspirations and 'language' of men in a bid to improve their social status and, therefore, the traditional 'masculine' traits remain universalised as 'human'. Further, when women do assume the behaviours, aspirations and 'language' of men they are criticized severely for being, for example 'the assertive manager' or a 'ladette'. The negative valuation of patriarchal notions of femininity has been left unquestioned and further, although women have entered the world of production, women's reproductive roles have continued to be devalued. Implicitly, then in an androgynous vision of an alternative society, masculine qualities, behaviours and attributes have continued to be valorised to the detriment of feminine qualities.

Within education this construction of gender where masculinity and femininity are cultural, therefore learned norms, was pivotal in enabling access to education challenging ideas of a gender differentiated curriculum and ensuring women's and girls' access to subjects which were traditionally deemed to be 'masculine' subjects such as science and mathematics and for which women and girls had been seen as less able to deal with because of the demands for rational thinking. However, the education of girls and women based on this construction of gender is geared towards preparing women to act in a 'man's world' – the educational process is designed to enable women to acquire those traits, behaviours, bodies of knowledge, capabilities associated with masculinity in order to be successful in the public domain. Further, in this construction of gender, women, who succeed in education academically or in relation to a career as an educational professional (in any sphere other than in areas of education for young children), were positioned as exceptional thereby not disrupting the privileging of masculinity. This led to the view that ultimately equal rights had had little impact on the distribution of power in patriarchal gender relations and consequently on the lives and educational opportunities of women. The question then becomes one of how to construct an educative process which validates women?

WOMAN-CENTRED APPROACHES

The limitations of the early equal rights position led to a challenge to the primacy of the attributes and values of masculinity. From this there emerged woman-centred position, particularly a form of radical feminism known as cultural feminism, which proposes that women possess exceptional and positive qualities which could change society for the better. In second wave of feminism, especially in writings from the women's peace movement and in academic disciplines such as psychology and theology, a significant theme is the reclamation and celebration of qualities, attributes and behaviours previously dismissed as merely 'feminine'. The traditional negative connotations attached to femininity are inverted and therein lie the seeds of social and political change. The subordinate position of women, instead of limiting women, becomes a resource in the process of social and political change. The psychologist, Jean Baker Miller (1986), for example, argues that from a powerless position women acquire the ability to question and subvert the ideologies of patriarchy in which power and dominance ensure success and prestige. She claims that women, by virtue of these subordinate roles they currently play, are psychologically more flexible and responsive, the qualities needed to bring humanity back from the brink of destruction. From their common experience of subordination, women will seek to empower rather than dominate others and this shapes the roles women play including that of educator.

As the phrase suggests, 'woman-centred approaches' is an umbrella term covering a diverse number of strands. While it is important to stress the plurality of approaches in this second phase, nevertheless there were two of the dominant themes: firstly, women's role as mothers and secondly, women's relationships with each other within a heterosexual economy. In contrast to the equal rights position in feminism, where efforts are concentrated on women gaining entry to the public domain including education, in this second phase, what were previously deemed personal issues have come into focus. Significantly, in debates about women's maternal role and women's sexuality, the possibilities for sociopolitical change are considered and so these themes are clearly evident in feminist utopian writing.

Similarly, Adrienne Rich in her non-fictional work *Of Woman Born* (1977), for example, suggests that women have qualities from their experiences of being mothers that must be valued in the public domain. A corresponding theme, found in many of the writings of the women's peace movement, is of women as 'life-bearers' who value life and peace. Sara Ruddick (1990) argues that women are the natural leaders of a new social order that will bring humanity back from the edge of nuclear disaster. The reclamation and celebration of traditional behaviours and experiences of women allows for some interrogation of patriarchal values. For Ruddick the task here is, firstly, to define and extol the virtues of 'true femininity' in terms of maternity and secondly, to use these virtues as the basis of a new social order which will replace the political and social systems of patriarchy. The transformed society would be based on the maternal values of nurturing and connectedness. A woman-centred position where motherhood is valued does have considerable potency: a reclaimed notion of femininity which is understood as lifegiving, peaceful, empowering could be the founding concept of a eutopia (good society). Women would be leaders in a eutopia founded on these principles; women would empower rather than exploit others, women as nurturers would establish ways of living that would counter the conflictual individualism of western patriarchal capitalism and women as mothers, as 'life bearers', would be the peacemakers.

This idea of constructing an alternative society based on principles associated with women's maternal role is a significant theme within feminist utopian writing. In this formulation of what it means to be a woman, learning is centred on experiences of nurturing and being nurtured. The primary relationship is that between mother and child. However, foregrounding mothering and motherhood in women's lives can be dangerously reductive of their potential. In Vonarburg's

(1992) *In Mothers' Land* set in a post nuclear holocaust world where women's fertility has been reduced to low levels, education is there to support a society stratified on the basis of women's reproductive capabilities. This utopian text helps to raise the question about how far should women's caring roles influence the educative process both as educators and as learners.

The other major theme in this second phase of feminism is the issue of women's sexuality as the defining feature in the construction of a better world for women. One of the earliest documents to emerge from the Women's Liberation Movement, *The Woman-Identified Woman* (1970/97) by the Radicalesbians, rejects patriarchal notions of 'true femininity', the core of which is a heterosexual relationship. Instead, new definitions that will ensure women are truly liberated must come from women's relationships with each other: "It is very difficult to realize and accept that being 'feminine' and being a whole person are irreconcilable. Only women can give to each other a new sense of self. That identity we have to develop with reference to ourselves, and not in relation to men. This consciousness is the revolutionary force from which all else will follow, for ours is an organic revolution... Our energies must follow toward our sisters, not backward toward our oppressors" (hypertext p 1). In this essay the Radicalesbians politicize what, in patriarchal ideologies is simply a matter of dysfunctional psychosexual development by arguing that it is only by becoming woman-identified that women can seek some kind of social improvement. This essay, which combines political analysis with a speculative element, is an important text in the development of debates about gender and social transformation. The essay is also illustrative of an important dynamic within woman-centred feminist theory, the focus on women's experiences and roles and the revaluing of these.

Women's bodies which, in a patriarchal society, are valued only in terms of the functions they serve for men – as sexual objects or as mothers – are to be reclaimed by women themselves as objects of desire to become the source of women's liberation. The project of writers such as Mary Daly (1979) is not to revalue the dominant patriarchal notions of femininity but to formulate new meanings. In a similar vein, Ruddick (1990) proposes that from their experience of motherhood, women acquire modes of thought different to those of men and from which they develop their potential for peace. Carol Gilligan (1982), a feminist psychologist, also argues that women, from their experience of being carers, acquire a specific 'feminine' moral sense that is based on connectedness with others. Further, the central role that relationships play in women's lives is seen to have a profound effect on how women think and learn. The project of reshaping meaning and exploring how women think and learn has important implications for education. Firstly, there is the question of what counts as valid knowledge in an educative process and secondly, how should women be engaged as learners?

DIFFERENCE AND WHAT IT MEANS TO BE A WOMAN

Within the second phase proposed by Kristeva, the pivotal construct is that of 'difference' defined in terms of sex difference that is irreducible. The second phase rests on a notion of 'woman' that is universal and so in efforts to reorder society, any differences between women are viewed as being less significant. This position, though, is disputed as it can lead to a construction of an educative process for women/girls that lacks an appreciation or a responsiveness to the impact of other factors on women accessing or participating in an engaged way in education. Writing within French feminist politics where, at that historical point the question of racial identity was less significant, Kristeva does not consider the emergence of debates and political activity around the issue of difference between women in her development in her schema of three phases. Nevertheless, it is important to consider how the question of difference between women is dealt with in feminist utopian writing and the implications of this for the construction of the educative process.

Within feminism, there was considerable debate about the potential and limitations of viewing women as homogeneous group what Firestone (1979) in her radical feminist utopian text, *The Dialectic of Sex,* called 'sex-class'. Defining women in terms of their shared characteristics and using this as a basis for a radical politics of social change denies the impact of other social factors such as social class, disability and race on women's lives and on the distribution of power within patriarchal society. The development of identity politics marked an important shift in feminist thought in both the USA and Great Britain, a critical dimension of which was the development of coalitions across different social groups seeking to bring about sociopolitical change.

Some of the first challenges to the dominant women-centred approaches came from women from minority groups, initially particularly African-American women, claiming that their group's distinctiveness from other women would need to be acknowledged in any politics of liberation for women. Writers such as bell hooks and Patricia Collins (1990) pointed to black women's experiences of oppression including their subjugation by white women. The emergence of black feminism as a significant position in the early 1980s questioned the foundation of a politics of change on a monolithic concept of 'woman'. An important aspect in black feminist thought is the attempt to conceptualise the multifaceted nature of women's identities.

In the writings of black feminists such as bell hooks we can see attempts to make visible the dynamic connections between different social factors such as social class and race as well as gender in women's experiences of oppression in a patriarchal society, and the implications of the multifaceted nature of women's identities for sociopolitical change. In the introduction of her book, *Ain't I a Woman* (1982), bell hooks writes:

> From the outset of my involvement with the women's movement I was disturbed by the white women's liberationists' insistence that race and sex were two separate issues. My life experience had shown me that the two issues were inseparable, that at the moment of my birth, two factors determined my destiny, my having been born black and my having been born female (p 12).

One of the major concerns in relation to woman-centred approaches is not just the erasure of differences between women but the political implications of conceiving women as a homogeneous group. The Combahee River Collective in *A Black Feminist Statement* (1998), written in 1979, highlight the dangers of definition when the notion of woman is premised on biological make up: "as Black women we find any type of biological determinism a particularly dangerous and reactionary basis upon which to build a politics" (p 523). The works of bell hooks illustrate the contribution of black feminist thought to feminist theory in highlighting the connections between gender and other social factors in women's experiences of oppression. In relation to feminist utopian writing hooks moves beyond difference simply in terms of racial or ethnic differences and helps to bring into focus the handling of a broader understanding of 'difference' in these writings.

Women-centred approaches encourage us re-conceptualise the educative process around changed definitions of what it means to be a woman from which have emerged discussions about feminist pedagogy and the ways women think and learn. However, these developments highlight the need for an appreciation of not only the impact of gender differences on women in education but differences between women that have a material effect on women's educational progress. Further, they suggest that bodies of knowledge based on 'women's lives and experiences' may be partial and that pedagogic practices based on a perceived commonality of women need to be interrogated in terms of power relationships between different groups of women.

Whereas in the second phase identified by Kristeva the question of what it means to be a woman is a founding idea in the development of a better society, the increasing emphasis by writers such as bell hooks on the need to recognise the impact of a range of social factors makes this a difficult question, due partly to the problems of finding a sufficiently flexible definition to encompass all women. This signals the wider dangers of seeking a universal definition because if women are defined by either biological make up or sexuality such a definition assumes an essentialist basis for what it means to be a woman. Defining women in these terms results in the conflation of gender with sex rather than treating gender as a social construct. Debates about what it means to be a woman have become polarised into two mutually exclusive positions: 'social constructionist' versus 'essentialist' and it is in the attempts to resolve the difficulties posed by this polarised debate that we can see the antecedents of what Kristeva conceives of as the third phase of feminism.

THE THIRD PHASE: THE NOT YET BECOME

In the third phase that Kristeva postulates, she argues that the notion of bipolar sex differences is redundant as a political tool on which to base a politics of social change: "What can 'identity', or even 'sexual identity', mean in a new theoretical and scientific space where the very notion of identity is challenged?'' (p 458). It is in theoretical writings such as Judith Butler's (1990, 1993) works on gender, that we see the ideas suggested by Kristeva as constituting the third stage of feminism beginning to be sketched out. Butler (1990) problematizes the assumption implicit in both the social constructionist and essentialist positions: that it makes sense to refer to a concept of 'woman' in order to make representational claims for the reconstruction of society. Butler, writing within North American feminism, takes on both the issues raised by identity politics as developed in the USA since the early 1980s as well as the polarised debate between social constructionism and essentialism.

Butler problematizes the notion of 'woman', first by examining the difficulties of perceiving 'women' as the subject of feminism and then by 'troubling' or deconstructing the concept of gender. An assumption in feminism is that there is a category of women, who by virtue of the fact that they are 'women', share common goals and interests which are represented through feminist politics. This assumption implies that there is a stable category of women, and, in Butler's view, this only leads to the further entrenchment of women in a subordinate position because they are still maintained as different: as 'not men' because women cannot occupy a subject position in patriarchy. Butler rejects any suggestion that the way to improve women's position is simply to reverse the values placed on male and female for this would still maintain: "... the categories of identity that contemporary juridical structures engender, naturalise and immobilise.." (p 5). What she proposes is a more profound change and rejects the view that the categories of gender are stable, 'natural' and unchanging; these categories instead are discursive formations. Through what she terms her genealogical critique, Butler seeks to 'trouble' the gender categories which support the differential positions of male and female and entrench heterosexuality as the 'natural' and only form of sexual relationship.

As a first step Butler rejects the notion that gender has any ontological basis. It is important to recognise that Butler is not simply maintaining the separation of the concepts of sex and gender which was crucial to the claim for equal rights, but instead probes more fundamentally the operation of the concepts of 'sex', and 'gender'. In the equal rights position, gender is seen as the cultural response to biological sex differences. This conceptualisation seems to imply that, because there is corporeality, sex already exists in/on the body. The figure of the body is, as Butler argues, being conceived of as "...mute, prior to culture, awaiting signification" (p 147). Butler disputes this conceptualisation of gender and seeks to illustrate the cultural apparatus and power regimes which constantly cite immutable sex differences to define gender. In patriarchal ideologies there is the presupposition of an essential sex which restricts the legitimacy of any other configuration of gender than that of masculinity and femininity. The power regimes that perpetuate these ideologies within a hegemonic order do so by presupposing an essential sex to which 'true' femininity or masculinity are inexorably linked. Instead of conceptualising gender as the cultural shaping of behaviour and expectation premised on immutable sex differences, Butler defines gender in a much more dynamic way: "...gender is an identity, tenuously constituted in time, instituted in an exterior space through a stylized repetition of acts" (p 140). By viewing gender in this way, Butler reverses the hierarchy and suggests that gender is the discursive means by which 'sexed nature' is given an ontological basis. Gender is performance: through language and social exchange, through repetitive signifying that is regulated by the discourses of patriarchy, gender identity is performed and regulated as normative.

Constructing gender as performance implies a sense of agency from which there is the possibility of challenging the dominant ideals of patriarchy. Butler points to the radical significance of the parody of gender used in drag and in political activities associated with queer politics. Here there is the subversion of 'normal' sexuality and gender in a humorous and ironic conceptualisation of female and male identity. However, even with the potentially useful conceptualisation of gender as performance, there are still a number of issues remaining. Butler addresses two of these questions in *Bodies that matter* (1993): firstly, there is the question of the materiality of the body in relation to the performativity of gender and secondly, there is the issue of how the concept of 'sex' relates to this understanding of the concept of 'gender'.

The relationship between the materiality of the body, gender performativity and the concept of sex is critical because if we do not map out these relationships there is the temptation to conceive gender performativity as a deliberative but momentary, transient act by an individual, akin to choosing a set of clothes, in which case any political underpinnings of the concept of 'gender' would be lost. One of the significant attractions of the concept of 'gender performativity' is the implication of agency, but if gender as performance is reduced to a process of simply 'donning' a gender without reference to hegemonic discourses, this immediately forecloses any opportunities available to reveal and thereby be able to challenge the power regimes that police behaviour and expectations.

The inadequacy of conceptualising gender as performativity in the narrow sense is immediately apparent as it does not take into account current understandings of gendered subjectivities; how can a subject simply 'don' a gender when 'its' existence is already decided by gender? Instead we need to consider more carefully what Butler means when she describes gender as "a stylised repetition of acts" (1990, p 140) in order to be able to both reveal the regimes of power that perpetuate and regulate gender while, at the same time, place agency within this understanding of gender. Thus, Butler (1993) argues that performativity is not a single act but instead is "...that reiterative power of discourse to produce the phenomena that it regulates and constrains" (p 2).

Gender, then, is significant within patriarchy as a set of stylized acts being constantly repeated as a set of discursive practices. However, we are still left with the question of how this relates to the category of sex. The idea that there is a prediscursive sex is one that appears accessible because it seems to be grounded in 'fact'; sex differences can be seen as a matter of material differences visible on and in the body. However, there are problems with the idea that there is a prediscursive sex that acts as a stable reference point on which and in relation to which cultural constructions of gender proceed. How can something be intelligible if it lies beyond the boundaries of discourse which mark what has cultural intelligibility within the existing regimes of power? Sex, therefore, is not simply a feature of the body but instead the 'sex' of the body is materialized through the repetitive norms that regulate gender within patriarchy. As Butler writes "...bodies only appear, only endure, only live within the productive constraints of highly gendered regulatory schemas" (1993, p xi). Through the constant repetition of normative practices that comprise gender, the sex of the body is materialised and becomes comprehensible within the power regimes of patriarchal society, that is within a male dominated heterosexual regime which marks the body as either male or female. That there is a need for constant repetition of regulatory gender practices suggests that materialisation is never fully complete, bodies do not live up to the ideas of gender within patriarchy, that is, to the ideal of 'true' femininity or masculinity. And so, Butler claims it is here that gaps and instabilities can appear which allow resistance and challenge to these ideologies of femininity and masculinity.

The way ahead for women would then be to reject the concept of 'woman' and the normative behaviour implied by this: "The loss of gender norms would have the effect of proliferating gender configurations, destabilizing substantive identity, and depriving the naturalizing narratives of compulsory heterosexuality of their central protagonists: 'man' and 'woman'" (Butler 1990 p 146). However, bodies that do not conform to the binary regime are not recognised as human within patriarchal discourse and are excluded: "[t]hese excluded sites come to bound the 'human' as its constitutive outside, and to haunt those boundaries as the persistent possibility of their disruption and rearticulation" (p 8).

IMAGING A DOMAIN OF ABJECTION

The idea that sex is a cultural norm which governs the materialisation of bodies is very potent because it enables us to challenge not only the ideals of femininity and masculinity but also, more profoundly, to challenge the idea of indissoluble sex differences between women and men, the founding idea of patriarchy. Sex is not then a prediscursive given but is assumed as part of the process of the formation of subjectivity. Butler argues that subject formation requires "...an identification with the normative phantasm of 'sex'" (p 3) which in patriarchal society is in terms of either male or female, these being mutually exclusive. Being a normative phantasm or illusion, it is an ideal that regulates, but an ideal that can be challenged and resisted. The formation of a subject requires identification with this illusory ideal of sex and this identification occurs by repudiating that which does not conform to the ideal. The repudiation vital for identification though creates excluded sites, what we could conceive of as domains of abjection. Any idea of a domain of abjection will be constantly denied, the focus will remain on regulating the process of identification within the normative pattern of patriarchy. Despite the denial of its existence, a domain of abjection will expose the artificiality of the ideals upon which the sexed subject has been identified. The abject questions the legitimacy of the founding presumptions of patriarchy of a society based on two sexes with primacy given to the male.

As Butler argues, although repudiation is essential to identification, that which is repudiated is denied. Thus, in patriarchal discourses the existence of anything other than two distinct and immutable sexes is constantly disclaimed. The disruptive potential of the existence of bodies that do not conform to the patriarchal two-sex regime, that is male and female, questions the underlying presumptions that legitimise bodies within this regime. However, the position of bodies that do not conform to the two-sex regime as sites of resistance is something that is disputed within feminist theory. Whether those bodies that do not fit into either category within the binary system, such as bodies that possess some of the characteristics of both sexes (transgender) or change from one sex to another (transsexual) can be regarded as transgressive is an issue debated within feminist theory and feminist utopian fiction.

THE CONCEPT OF GENDER AND THE EDUCATIVE PROCESS

In this conceptualisation of gender we can see Butler articulating ideas that could become the basis of the 'Not Yet Become' a society in which the binary gender regime underpinning patriarchal society is no longer influential. Eutopia, the good society, from this position, would be a society in which gender is no longer the determinant of the order of that society because there are multiple or unstable genders. The idea of woman which maintains the idea of "...a scapegoat victim as foundress of a society or counter-society..." (Kristeva 1991 p 459) is redundant as a founding concept. The focus is not on the 'nature' of the individual but on the multiple possible positions an individual could occupy, as Kristeva suggests, the purpose of feminism is: "…to bring out the singularity of each woman, and beyond this, her multiplicities, her plural languages…" (p 458). In a eutopia founded on this position, being biologically male or female would have no social significance and would not determine social position and power nor would it determine gender of which there could be endless fluidity.

We can turn to both fictional and non-fictional feminist utopian writing to begin to perceive glimpses of what a world in which gender has no sociopolitical significance might be like. In *A Manifesto for Cyborgs Science, Technology and Socialist Feminism in the 1980s* (1990) Haraway proposes the partial identity of cyborgs can help us to understand what a post-gendered world would be like and by writing stories we can explore these ideas. Haraway looks to fiction as the means of developing ideas for a cyborg politics for women: "…storytellers exploring what it means to be embodied in high-tech worlds" (p 216). This is an idea that has been taken up in other speculative feminist works which anticipate the increasing influence of technology especially digital technologies through which different virtual realities. These works allows us to consider not just whether a gender-free educative process is possible but, is it desirable.

In the theoretical works such as Judith Butler's writings we begin to find the proposal for the third stage suggested by Kristeva of a world in which binary gender is no longer a fundamental factor in the construction of society. It would be easy to dismiss Butler's discussion of the concepts of 'sex' and 'gender' as being far removed from the material realities of the classroom, schools and other educational institutions. Gender remains a significant factor in shaping the educational experiences and achievements of learners. What Butler challenges us to consider is the use of a bi-polar construction of gender with mutually exclusive categories which in turn constructs gender policy in education as two distinct sets of competing needs to be addressed.

SUMMARY

Kristeva's utopian essay *Women's Time* has provided us with a framework to map out three competing ideas in relation to the construction of 'gender'. This discussion raises three fundamental questions about educational policy and practice that underpin the exploration of these themes which I will return to in the final chapter. Should the task in education be one of ensuring gender equality with education as it is currently conceived and constructed or should it be about reforming the educative process that it takes as a central concern the experiences of women and of other minority groups who historically have been marginalized? Or should we seek to create a gender-free educational process, if indeed this is possible?

In addition to these broad questions about the significance of the concept of gender in education, a number of themes relating to education have emerged from this discussion. The three key themes that I will consider are:

1. the role of experience in the generation of knowledge and the development of pedagogic practice: do women have a distinctive way of thinking;
2. the construction of educating and learning in terms of women's caring roles;
3. the impact of social and technological trends on the issue of gender in the educational process.

CHAPTER 5

CONSCIOUSNESS RAISING: KNOWLEDGE AND PEDAGOGY

Introduction

As part of the utopian project of feminism to bring about social transformation to end the subjugation of women would no longer be oppressed, a range of practices were adopted such as alternative communes, gatherings of women (short and long term), the creation of women's spaces and later protest camps to develop praxis for change. Side by side with these developments has been an outpouring of feminist utopian writing, both fictional and non-fictional. In these discussions, areas of life both public and personal were held up for scrutiny and reform including education. Women reflected on their often alienating experiences of formal education but also looked to explore an educative process to create the conditions for political and social change through the agency of women: how and what might women learn to bring about sociopolitical change. Thus, discussions developed around issues related to what and how women learned which challenged established disciplinary knowledge and pedagogic practices. The roots of the development of 'new knowledge' and feminist pedagogy lie partly in the political activities of the early years of the Women's Liberation but the ideas and practices forged in this context continue to shape discussions about the educative process and social transformation.

In the early years of Women's Liberation in the late 1960s and 1970s – there grew, almost spontaneously, a political practice of women coming together in consciousness raising (CR) groups – or 'rap sessions' as they were sometimes called – to explore their experiences of what it means to be female living in a patriarchal society and to create alternative ways of living and new identities as women. CR was the subject of much discussion in the Women's Liberation Movement with a range of essays and articles theorising the process as well as providing advice about how to conduct CR groups in order that women can share their experiences and build theory for political change. This building of theory was also realised in fictional utopias including, for example, Joanna Russ's (1975) *The Female Man* and Sally Miller Gearhart's (1979) *The Wanderground.* Women's lived experiences are the core of CR where women's voices are privileged and where women telling their own stories becomes the core upon which theory and praxis for social and political change are based. MacKinnon (1989) positions CR as 'the feminist method' in the project of social transformation. CR might be characterized in Bloch's (1956) terms as the means by which 'Not-Yet-Conscious' hopes of change into 'Not-Yet-Become', ideas upon which to base political action.

Fundamentally, CR is both a utopian practice and an educative process by which 'new' knowledge and new ways of thinking about what it means to be a woman are generated and through which women come to understand existing unequal gender relations. A common outcome of such work within the Women's Liberation Movement was a significant discontent with an education system which seemed to reinforce patriarchal ideas about what it means to be a woman and thereby naturalising the structured inequalities between women and men. Although CR groups were established outside any formal education system, the legacy of CR was felt in the academy where women began to question the universal application of theories and practices derived from men's experiences and perceptions. Further, the practice of CR also raised questions about the marginal position occupied by women as learners within the educational system thus pointing to the need to develop an educative process that was based on knowledge drawn from women's characteristic experiences and which reflected women's distinctive approaches to learning.

CR, particularly in its earliest years, was based on the belief that women share common experiences within a patriarchal society. The analysis of these experiences led to a radical feminist ideology of "a female culture" (Burris, 1973, p 341) which asserts that women, regardless of what society they live in or what background they come from, share the same oppressive conditions. Given this, efforts were focused on revealing not only the regimes of power that keep women in a subordinate position but also delineating the distinctive qualities, attributes and abilities of women upon which an alternative and more equal social order might be developed. In this chapter I explore the way in which this ideological construction of gender, which privileges women's distinctiveness has shaped debates about both the generation of knowledge and pedagogic practice. In this chapter I explore the impact of feminist utopian thinking on two interrelated aspects of the educative process: the development of 'new knowledge' to challenge patriarchal ideologies and the development of feminist pedagogy to develop women's agency in their own learning as part of the enterprise of social transformation.

TELLING THEIR STORIES

The origins of consciousness raising (CR) in feminism lie in the Women's Liberation Movement where small groups of women came together to explore their common experiences of living in a male-dominated society. The idea of using people's lived experiences to explore oppression predates the Women's Liberation Movement, with similar strategies in evidence in other radical movements such as left wing groups of the 1960s, the Civil Rights movement in the USA and in liberatory approaches to education particularly Frierean pedagogy (Friere, 1972). Nevertheless this was a process that very much captured the imagination of the nascent women's liberation movement being a topic of considerable discussion evident from the range of published essays, articles and mimeographed papers on the subject written by women directly involved in the Women's Liberation Movement as well as finding expression in fictional works.

June Arnold (2000), who went on to write several feminist novels, described the development of the CR group she was involved in. What comes across from this essay is the empowering experience of being part the group: as trust amongst members of the group develops, women are able to explore their most intimate and often most painful experiences as well as their every day lives. However, the process of CR is more than emotional support. It is through this sharing of experiences the women come to the realisation that the problem is not caused by their individual shortcomings but is the result of structured inequalities. Further, by appreciating their subordinate role within patriarchal gender relations women can begin to forge political action to bring about change. The implications of this political analysis have been felt in all social formations including education. CONSCIOUSNESS-RAISING is not 'educational' in that there are no exams or competitive aims. "CONSCIOUSNESS-RAISING is '*educational*' in that it provides the support of other women and their recognition of us and what we have to say" (Women's Collective n.d., p 2, emphasis in the original).

CR also challenges understandings of what we mean by 'education': CR is fundamentally a learning process, the purpose of which is social transformation. From the analysis of their experiences and feelings women began to conceptualise their position within the unequal power relations of patriarchal society. In her essay with its iconic title, 'The Personal is Political', Hanisch (2000) argues: "one of the first things we discover in this group is that personal problems are political problems" (p 114). Sarachild's (2000) account of the development of CR in the Redstockings Group (a radical women's liberation group which continues to work in New York) provides a sense of the excitement of the women in developing CR.

> The idea was to take our feelings and experience more seriously than any theories which did not satisfactorily clarify them, and to devise new theories which did reflect the actual experience and feelings and necessities of women (p 6).

The writings on CR have a clear utopian stance: women telling of their own stories is a political act, the starting point in bringing about social change. This idea of the political power of women's stories was taken up in the growing body of feminist fictional utopias.

The Wanderground (Gearhart, 1979) is a key work within the canon of contemporary feminist utopian fiction written as a result of the ferment of the Women's Liberation Movement and the writer's own political activities within gay and lesbian politics. Although there are strong elements of fantasy in this novel, *The Wanderground* was influential as much for its form as for its content, the work being a series of stories told by different women about their lives under the increasingly extreme male-dominated society of the City. It is by bringing together these stories and mapping out common threads that the power regimes of patriarchal gender relations are revealed which then provides the basis for the political action necessary to bring about social transformation.

> Decades ago each woman who had escaped to the hills had offered – usually with great pain – the memory of her city experience, however dramatic or

> mild, however heroic or horror-ridden. Her experience as she had known it had been added then to the vessels of memory kept within the person of every Hill woman. 'Lest we forget how we came here'. From the countless seemingly disconnected episodes the women had pieced together a larger picture so that now they had some sense of what had happened during those last days in the City. Over the years as women had joined them the memory vessels had been added to: more and more stories, more and more horrors, and sometimes a narrative that brought with it some hope or humour. As a woman shared, she becomes part of all their history (p 24).

THE EDUCATIVE PROCESS OF CONSCIOUSNESS RAISING

Very quickly the process of CR was itself the subject of theorisation with Allen (1973) providing a conceptual framework outlining the four stages of development of CR groups. The process begins with opening up where women in a supportive environment can relate their experiences and feelings of both major aspects of their lives and seemingly trivial incidents. At this stage what is important is that "someone listens and does not ridicule; someone listens and acknowledges the validity of another's view of her life" (p 274) in a non-judgemental space. The next stage is to move onto sharing where "the emphasis is on teaching one another through sharing experiences" (p 275). It is through listening to each other's stories and then drawing these experiences together that the women come to realise the political roots of the problem and so move "...to finding the real causes of these problems rather than merely emphasizing one's own inadequacies" (p 275). The location of the problem is then critically important. Sarachild (2000) argues that "the importance of listening to a woman's feelings was collectively to analyze the situation of women, *not to analyze her*" (p 6 italics in original). The objective in this phase is to demonstrate the commonality between women's experiences.

The CR group then engages in the third stage, analysis, at which point new ideas are generated to explain not only women's oppression but to frame ways of challenging the status quo. What takes place now is "...the development of concepts which attempt to define not only the why's and how's of our oppression but ways of fighting that oppression" (p 276). The task of analysing is potentially difficult as many women had been denied access to experiences that enabled them to develop their ability to conceptualise. Other sources of ideas, for example, books, can come into play but, in Allen's view, it is critically important that any analysis must come after the two preceding stages of opening up and sharing so the generation of ideas and concepts is about explaining women's experiences rather than fitting these experiences into pre-conceived ideas reflecting normative patriarchal thinking. The final stage that Allen maps out is that of abstracting, the stage her own group had reached at the time of writing this essay. Here there is the development of 'Free Space' (p 278) in which the group is beginning to appreciate the impact of social institutions on women's experiences and to develop specific concepts and ideals on which to base theories and actions for change. Allen highlights both the personally enriching quality of CR groups as well as this clear political nature particularly as the group extrapolate principles from their experiences in order to develop of political theory. "Intellectually this is the most exciting stage. It is a joy to learn to think, to begin to comprehend what is happening to us. Ideas are experiences in themselves, freeing, joyous experiences which give us the framework for formulating our actions" (p 278). Similarly, Sarachild (1978) highlights this key characteristic of focusing on women's collective experiences from which they could generate understanding and theories to support political action:

> The idea was to take our feelings and experience more seriously than any theories which did not satisfactorily clarify them, and to devise new theories which did reflect the actual experience and feelings and necessitates of women (p 6).

Allen and Sarachild both provide a conceptual analysis of the process of consciousness raising. There were numerous other publications, both published essays and more ephemeral mimeographed papers, which laid out guidelines and 'curricula' for these groups. In a paper written for the Cape Cod Women's Liberation Organization, Piercy and Freeman (1972), for example, provide guidance on the setting up and organising a group and a list of possible topics for discussion. Similarly in *How to start your own consciousness-raising group*, The Chicago Women's Liberation Union (1971) lists possible questions on women's experiences in relation to a wide ranging set of topics including marriage, sex, femininity, child care, housework as well as women's history. Specific practices in running a group are also outlined such as turn taking, no formal leadership, women-only and participation by all. From these writings there is a strong sense of enthusiasm; CR was initially a very dynamic and exhilarating experience in which many women came to articulate a political realisation of their subordinate position. In Hoegeland's (1998) view, however, CR groups became highly conventionalised over the decade of the 1970s. There was a gradual falling-off of groups whose primary function was consciousness raising with groups instead tending to cohere around specific projects or issues. However, CR left a legacy in the continuing debates in two areas: in discussions about the relationship between the construction of knowledge and women's experiences and in the development of pedagogies intended to enable empower women.

THE CONSTRUCTED NATURE OF KNOWLEDGE

CR groups were a significant feature of the early years of the development of second wave feminism and acted as a starting point for discussions about the nature and generation of knowledge. In her influential work, MacKinnon (1989) considers consciousness raising as the core of feminism: as dialectics is 'the marxist method', consciousness raising is 'the feminist method'. She defines consciousness-raising as "the collective critical reconstitution of the meaning of women's social experience' (p 83). CR is deeply embedded in the collective and material realities of women's lives but at the same time exposes the ideological regimes that determine the social and political positioning of women. Theory is built on the analysis of women's lived experience.

The initial impetus for CR groups was based on the view that women have something broadly in common but MacKinnon argues that what becomes evident from CR, is that this "working assumption becomes a working discovery: women are a group, in the sense that a shared reality of treatment exists sufficient to provide a basis for identification" (p 86). The critical concept here is the shared nature of the experiences of what it means to be a woman "simply being a woman has a meaning that decisively defines all women socially, from their most intimate moments to their most anonymous relations" (p 90). MacKinnon argues that male power is perpetuated by means of hidden but self-reinforcing ideological workings. Thus any sense of alienation that a woman might experience as a result patriarchal gender relations is constructed as a problem of maladjustment located within the individual woman. The ideologies of gender that maintain structured inequalities remain hidden. CR enables women to appreciate the operation of these regimes of power in both the private and the public domains. What CR collectively gather women's experiences both seemingly trivial or fleeting moments as well as more substantial experiences and then "coheres and claims these impressions" (p 85).

CR then has implications both for epistemology as well as politics: CR is 'lived knowing' (p 95). The epistemological starting point within feminism is to MacKinnon's mind, different from that of science or even social science. In science the search is for objective truth that exists 'out there'; in social science, social experience is problematic as the basis for knowledge – the knower will distort or interpret social reality so the knower creates a barrier to the known. In contrast, feminist practice "redefines the epistemological issue from being the scientific one, the relation between knowledge and objective reality, to a problem of the relation of consciousness to social being" (p 99). By exploring not just what they know, but how they know, women are able to analyse some of the ideological workings that define what it means to be a woman within a patriarchal sociopolitical order. The purpose of CR is not to delineate 'a body of knowledge' in disciplinary terms but to develop 'a way of knowing'. Feminist epistemology challenges the 'in here' and 'out there' dichotomy perpetuated by scientific and rational discourse.

There is a question of why CR is seen as so transformative: substantial evidence can be derived from empirical studies of women's subordinate position but this 'knowledge' does not have the same impact on women as the process of engaging in CR. The purpose is not to produce an 'objective' body of knowledge or to present a 'perfect reflection of the reality' but instead to construct knowledge on the basis of the women's collective lived experiences. It is through constructing an alternative epistemology in which social and political change can be envisioned that women can set aside what they have been conditioned to believe and instead act and work for social and political change.

WHAT DOES A WOMAN NEED TO KNOW?

As MacKinnon (1989) argues, CR exposed existing unequal gender relationships by revealing the ideological workings of power regimes. Through this process women were also encouraged to appreciate the constructed nature of knowledge. Men are the producers of knowledge: they dominate the roles of researchers, theoreticians, scholars and experts; they generate knowledge about women but this knowledge reflects their own perceptions and positions as men within the structured inequalities of patriarchal relations. Women's role in the generation of knowledge tended to be limited to that of being the object of study rather than as generators of knowledge. Often studies based on men's lives are assumed to have universal application and, where women's experiences are included, these are seen through the lens of male experience and authority. In the disciplines of knowledge on which curricular were based, there was no authentic exploration of women's experiences.

Adrienne Rich (1986a), whose poetry and prose has been influential in feminist theory, asks the question 'what does a woman need to know'? For Rich 'knowing' is about a woman's self definition and awareness of oneself. There has been a denial or simply neglect of women's history and of women's continued subordination within patriarchal gender relations which has helped to reinforce women's subordination but as Rich argues, "...not anatomy, but enforced ignorance, has been crucial to our powerlessness" (p 2). Thus, women need to know about the social and political position of women, about women's history including women who have risen above the marginalized positions, about the politics of the female body. With this knowledge women can challenge social formations that perpetuate women's subordinate roles. Women – even relatively privileged women – can also come to appreciate that heterosexuality within patriarchal gender relations reifies male power. In this address to a group of women about to graduate, Rich cautions that women must maintain their sense of the experience of marginalisation:

> It was only when I could finally affirm the outsider's eye as a source of legitimate and coherent vision, that I began to be able to do the work I truly wanted to do, live the kind of life I truly wanted to live (p 3).

These ideas are not simply about individual betterment which will allow exceptional or privileged women to progress but instead are about provoking action towards social transformation through which women as a group can begin to dismantle the power regimes that place them in subordinate roles. Their 'outsider's eye' provides them with a critical perspective that not only validates their lives but enables them to read the workings of the power regimes within patriarchal gender relations.

There is, however, a difficulty in looking to women's subordinated role as the source of their knowledge, that shapes their way of knowing. To claim distinctiveness is to potentially reinforce the marginalized position of women: not only are women's ways of knowing different from men's ways of knowing but these are derived from their powerless state. This viewpoint has the potential to reinforce oppressive gender relations placing women outside the regimes of power. Rich (1987b), in an essay *Toward a Woman-Centred University* calls for:

> A reorganisation of knowledge, of perspectives and analytical tools that can help us to know our foremothers, evaluate our present historical, political, and personal situation, and take ourselves seriously as agents in the creation of a more balanced culture (p 141).

Rich is anticipating here not only the challenge to existing biased bodies of knowledge but also to explanations of how women think. It is not just 'what' a women needs to know but 'how' a woman knows. Feminism has had a significant impact on disciplinary knowledge. Work began on this in the early stages of feminism particularly in the area of psychology with works such as Jean Baker Miller's (1986) *Towards a New Psychology of Women* and Carol Gilligan's (1982) study of women's moral thinking, *In a Different Voice.* Gilligan's work challenged Laurence Kolhberg's (1981) stages of moral development, the epitome of which was to deal with moral dilemmas on rational grounds of principle. Gilligan argues that the way Kohlberg had analysed the moral reasoning of his female subjects does not reflect the way women engage in moral dilemmas. In her study Gilligan demonstrated that women have a distinctive way of thinking about moral dilemmas based on relationships rather than abstract principle. Gilligan's work pointed the way to another highly influential study of the wider question of women's epistemological development by Belenky, Clinchy, Goldberger, and Tarule (1986) published as *Women's Ways of Knowing*.

WOMEN'S WAYS OF KNOWING

There are many resonances between principles underpinning CR and the study, *Women's Ways of Knowing*. Belenky et al. argue that, up to that point, theories of development were based on male samples and experiences particularly those relating to intellectual development which reinforced male/female, thinking/ emotions polarities. To challenge this position, their study explores and schematizes women's intellectual capabilities. Belenky et al. drew from a previous study by Perry (1970) who had used a sample of undergraduates at Harvard to chart epistemological development. Belenky et al. were critical of the bias in the developmental schema charted by Perry as it was based on the analysis of data from male subjects and so typifies the tendency to overlook the possible distinctiveness of women's modes of knowing and thinking.

The ethnographic methodology of this groundbreaking work reflects the feminist stance of the work in order to give women the opportunity to tell their story about how they know and learn and indeed, how they have been frequently silenced within different contexts. There is a constant emphasis on women's voice: the text is rich with the verbatim accounts provided by the women of their experiences. "The stories of these women drew us back into a kind of knowing that had too often been silenced by institutions in which we grew up and of which we were a part" (p 20).

Belenky et al. argue that many women feel marginalised or alienated from education which pursues areas that they do not see as relevant to their own concerns or relate to their development. Further, education reflects a male-dominated culture and "...little attention has been given to modes of learning, knowing and valuing that may be specific to, or at least common in women" (p 6). When women's voices and their experiences of being silenced are then admitted into the discourses of an educational setting, this can lead to profound change not just for the women involved but on what is constructed as 'knowledge'. Belenky et al. see the articulation of female values through women's voices, that is, the generation of knowledge from women's experiences as being transformative of ideas and subjects.

The embeddedness of the social and the collective in knowing is evident in each stage of this schema for the epistemology development of women. The schema charts the move from external where women's referents are others particularly those 'experts' in authority positions, to the internal where women's own experiences are valued, to then the connecting together of the inner and outer sources of knowledge:

> it is in the process of sorting out the pieces of the self and of searching for a unique and authentic voice that women come to the basic insights of constructivist thought – all knowledge is constructed and the knower is an intimate part of the known (p 137).

It is here that women understand their own agency as 'the knower' in constructing knowledge. As women develop as thinkers their own experiences rather than general propositions become the starting point. However, this is not to suggest that women reject or cannot work with abstraction to make sense of experience. Instead, as in CR principle and abstraction follow on from experience.

From their work Belenky et al. specify five epistemological perspectives in relation to women's development – how women know and view the world. These categories are (1) silence where women, frequently because of early experiences of neglect and isolation, express feelings of not having a voice nor even a conception of themselves as a learner and where all knowledge and authority is external to them and indeed often arbitrary in its impact on them; (2) received knowledge is where the voice of the other is privileged, where women still see knowledge as being derived from an external authority and where their task is to listen and retain this knowledge; (3) subjective knowledge where women begin to find their own voice which is "the hallmark of women's emergent sense of self and sense of agency and control" (p 69) and where experiences and social involvement are a source of knowledge though women here still distrust other more abstract ways of knowing; (4) procedural knowledge is 'knowing how' where women learn the ways of acquiring and demonstrating knowledge; (5) connected knowledge where women weave together strands of rational and emotive knowledge and integrate objective knowledge and subjective knowing.

Belenky et al. use their schema, particularly the category of silence to explore women's alienation from education. Including the category of 'silence' as a stage in epistemological development was a remarkable aspect of the study. Women's silence has become a motif within feminist theory but has had different treatments. Eagleton (2003) points to its subversive potential: that silence in the public forums would help conceal women's true knowledge and attributes, the hidden culture of women. However, in attributing 'silence' as a stage in a schema for the epistemological development of women, Belenky and her co-authors were clear that silence was the result of women's experiences of exclusion and deprivation and not a position to be celebrated.

> The bleak images that emerge from these stories suggest childhoods with neither much play or dialogue. Growing up without opportunities for play and for dialogue poses the gravest danger for the growing child (p 32).

Many of the other women reflected this feeling of being silenced, having nothing to contribute leading them to not see themselves as learners at all. In the study were women who were not involved in formal education and who were among the most deprived socially and economically. The "transformation of language to action" (Lorde, 1980, p 12) then becomes not just personally but politically transforming:

> My silences have not protected me. Your silence will not protect you. But for every real word spoken, for every attempt I had ever made to speak those truths for which I am still seeking, I had made contact with other women while we examined the words to fit a world in which we all believed, bridging our differences (Lorde, 1980, p 13).

WOMAN-CENTRED EDUCATION

Belenky et al.'s study helps underline that in women's education, centrally important is the relationship between how women see themselves – their self-concept – and their way of knowing and learning. The importance of recognising not just previous experiences of schooling but the wider social experiences which shape how a woman comes 'to know', how they learn and indeed, how they come to see themselves as capable of knowing and learning. For Belenky et al. "the quest for self and voice plays a central role in transformation in women's ways of knowing" (p 133). When the interviewees in the study by Belenky et al. were asked of their experience what emerges are themes that are "distinctively though not exclusively female" (p 191). These experiences have not been perceived as affirming and supportive of the women as capable learners.

Belenky et al.'s work illustrates that many women are alienated from the educational system in which curricula are based upon male-inscribed objective bodies of knowledge delivered in ways that privilege abstraction, rationality and objectivity. They argue instead for the distinctiveness of women's epistemological development with 'connected thinking' being a more readily attainable way of thinking for women than 'separate knowing'. Women's educational experiences, to their mind, should nurture the development of connected thinking: "education conducted on the connected model would help women toward, community, power and integrity" (p 228). One of the ways that feminists have tried to counter this is by developing alternative curricular programmes that reflect women's experiences: in ideas such as 'girl-friendly schooling' (Whyte et al., 1975) and particularly in the growth of Women's Studies (Jackson, 2004) as an area of scholarship taught in higher education and in continuing education. Nevertheless, Coffey and Delamont (2000) argue that there has been little reshaping of school curricula in the UK:

> The school, curriculum can be conceptualized as one in which dominant discourses seek to normalise some knowledges, and regulate or mute other knowledges. And with this conceptualization gender relations are enmeshed with the content and delivery of the curriculum (p 31).

Discussions about women's ways of knowing raise questions about whose experiences define curricula.

WHOSE STORIES?

Belenky et al. highlight the importance of women's experiences and awareness which enable them to become generators of knowledge. As McKenna (2001) argues the generation of the stories of their own lives not only enables women to build knowledge but "to develop critical and flexible habits of mind" (p 149). However, this raises the question of what can be defined as 'the female experience' – whose stories are to be considered accounts of authentic female experience? In *The Female Man* Russ (1985) illustrates the fundamental challenges in trying to construct a politics and social formations such as education around the notion of a definitive female experience. This novel explores the lives of four women who are the same genetic prototype and are identical physically so any differences are due to contrasting social experiences. There is Joanna from the contemporary world, Jeanine from a near future society where women continue to play a subordinate role, Janet from the all female eutopia of Whileaway and finally, Jael who lives a highly privileged life in a world where women and men are strictly segregated in two separate societies of Manland and Womanland. The sharp contrast between the opportunities for self-actualisation that Janet has had and those of Joanne point up what can be achieved with an educational process in which women's experiences are privileged. However, Jael's story asks us whether we should be valorising all experiences of women. Jael's story illustrates in horrific imagery women's capacity to oppress others.

In Manland although femininity is despised, women remain the objects of fascination and desire. The meeting between the Boss man and Jael moves from fascination with the 'unknown', to sexual desire to, finally, sheer hatred and contempt once Jael rejects violently both his advances and grandiose plans. At one level Jael's attack on this Manlander seems justified given his threatening behaviour; however there is a strong sense of unease about the episode. As Jael gets ready to strike the final blow the man continues on his tirade demonstrating the deep contempt women are held in:

> 'OPEN YOUR EYES!" I roared, 'BEFORE I KILL YOU!" and Boss-man did.
>
> He said, You led me on.
>
> He said, You are a prude. (He was shocked.)
>
> He said, You deceived me.
>
> He said, You are a Bad Lady
>
> (p 181, italics in the original).

In the sheer ferocity of her attack and her physical transformation, Jael displays equally brutish attributes. As she attacks the man the appearance of her claws is likened to his erection:

> Boss was muttering something angry about his erection so, angry enough for two, I produced my own – by this I mean that the grafted muscles on my fingers and hands pulled back the loose skin, with that characteristic itchy tickling, and of course, you are wise, you have guessed that I do not have cancer on my fingers but claws, talons like a cat's but bigger, a little more dull than wood brads but good for tearing. And my teeth are a sham over metal (p 181).

This is a horrific scene where Jael tears the Boss to shreds and we can understand the shock and repulsion of the other three women, Joanna, Janet and Jeannine who witness this scene. What places Jael as a brutal and depraved figure is her final comment: "I like it" (p 184). The arguments put forward for the role of the experience of women suggests that there is a definable and identifiable body of knowledge being generated from 'the female experience'. Russ, in both her depiction of the four women in this utopian novel, and particularly her portrayal of Jael, reminds us vividly of the huge diversity there is among women. Russ questions simplistic ideas of an authentic women's experience. Any understanding of the universal experience of women is deeply problematic in feminism.

WOMEN'S EXPERIENCE

A central idea in CR was the construction of women as a 'sex class' (Firestone, 1979) in which there were common experiences of oppression. However, as the decade of the 1970s progressed this position became under increasing attack as issue of difference between women emerged. Audrey Lorde speaking in 1979 was highly critical of academic feminism where difference was over looked arguing that such a denial perpetuates rather than challenges the existing power regimes.

> Those of us who stand outside the circle of society's definition of acceptable women; those of us who have been forged in the crucibles of difference – those of us who are poor, who are lesbians, who are Black, who are older –

> know that survival is not an academic skill. It is learning how to stand alone, unpopular and sometime reviled, and how to make common cause with those others identified as outside the structures in order to define and seek a world in which we can all flourish. It is learning how to take our differences and make them strengths. *For the master's tools will never dismantle the master's house.* They may allow us temporarily to beat him at his own game, but they will never enable us to bring about genuine change. And this fact is only threatening to those women who still define the master's house as their only sources of support (Lorde 1980 p159-160, italics in the original).

Stories of women's experience are potential learning processes but we need to expose the social and political practices, both cultural and familial, that have shaped these. A critical question is raised about whose experiences are voiced, whose experience is seen as being authoritative, which person or group of people can speak, who are silenced. We need to be careful not to see knowledge drawn from experience as any more truthful or authentic, or to suggest that it comes in a pure untainted form. This knowledge is constructed ideologically. There is a need in Fuss's (1989) view to balance the use of experiential knowledge with "a strong materialist analyses of the structural and institutional bases of exploitation" (p 117). Fuss argues that educators need to "negotiate the gap between the conservative fiction of experience as the ground of all truth-knowledge and the immense power of this fiction to enable and encourage student participation" (p 118).

For both students and teachers the historical situatedness of their experiences and their subjectivities may be contradictory and fluid. Claiming a universal set of experiences, then, may lead to conflict among learners and result in both a rejection of the idea of their own role in oppression and the internalisation of the ideologies of the dominant power regimes. The use, then, of women's experiences is a complex issue. On the one hand this approach has enormous potential in including and engaging women as learners but on the other hand such an approach can reinforce dualistic notions of gender. As Fuss (1989) suggests the emphasis on lived experience – on identity politics can "operate in the classroom both to authorize and de-authorize speech" (p 113) because "'female experience', is never as unified as knowable, as universal, as stable as we presume it to be" (p 114). Further, as Ryan (2001) challenges any attempt to construct a definitive account on epistemological grounds will: "preclude the possibility of moving out of or deconstruction or subverting dualism" (p 71).

FEMINIST PEDAGOGY

The use of women's experiences in the classroom then raises questions about pedagogy. Weiler (1991) seeks to situate feminist pedagogy in the growth of Women's Studies programmes in higher education where the experiences of consciousness raising were taken into the classroom. However, this has not been a simple translation of sets of practices from the informal and structureless context of consciousness raising groups to the regulated context of a university programme.

There are some critical questions about how the tenets of CR can form a pedagogy in an institutional setting particularly around issues of the role of the teacher and the engagement of all learners. The freewheeling approach characteristic of CR poses difficulties within an institutional setting.

Characteristically CR has a very limited structure, with no detailed agendas or any identifiable leaders. Arnold (2000) saw CR as testimony to women's ability to collaborate. The leaderless structure and women's ability to listen, to speak a common language were seen as core in enabling women to build a political analysis of their position in society. Thus in *The Wanderground* Gearhart's utopian novel, discussion, debate and dialogue are central to the sociopolitical processes of the community:

> Drawing her own presence to the centre of the gatherstretch, Li...brought the question before them. Li did not address an audience but instead herself became a hearer as she wove back and forth in her memory between narrative and reflection, description and evaluation, attempting to throw open to all women the information that had come...The sharing began – small tales and long tales of separate matters, each not so grave but when taken together lent an ominous tone to the last few months... There was a long but very full silence in the gatherstretch. No one moved to the centre, yet all listened to each other, to themselves. It was a time of assimilating, of understanding the news. Zephyr was aware of the raw emotions surrounding her, predominantly outrage and fear...Silence. Miraculous silence. The remembering of who they were. Tui. A moment for the hope of agreement. A moment for the readiness to struggle, a moment for the re-commitment to care, whatever the eventual outcomes would be. Gradually the presencing grew strong again. Some unity, bonding on a fundamental level struck an ultimate sense in every gather-stretching woman. It went as deep as their female nature and spread wide as their infinitely varied temperaments...All moved towards the gentle holding of two calm lakes, each one for the other (p 135-139).

This might seem fanciful but women's abilities in being able to communicate and collaborate are potent ideas in feminist thinking. This fictional vision of women communicating is resonated in Belenky et al's (1986) model of connected teaching. Teachers need to be transparent in their own thinking as they grapple with ideas so the learners appreciate not only is knowledge constructed but it is always partial and evolving. Further, teachers need to nurture the students in the forming and presenting of their own ideas. Thus in connected teaching both teachers and learners "engage in the process of thinking and they talk out what they are thinking in a public dialogue" (p 219).

Within the institutionalised setting of a classroom – particularly a classroom within an academic institution such as a college or university (where much of the development on feminist pedagogy has been undertaken and theorised) immediately the teacher/lecturer is positioned in authority as someone who designs, delivers and assesses the programme and so whose decisions will have consequences of the students. The demands of the academy impose structured power relationships in classrooms that did not exist in CR groups. Women as teachers wanting to adopt a feminist approach are faced with a dilemma. If, on the one hand, they continue with the 'acceptable' pedagogies based on the unequal relationship between teacher/active and learner/ passive, women teachers would be colluding in the perpetuation of the dominant power regimes. If, on the other hand, women negate the power invested in them as a teacher/lecturer they would be further marginalizing themselves and the growing body of feminist scholarship within the academy. Feminist educators looked to reshaping the teacher/student relationship and their pedagogic practices to recognise the agency of the students in building theory, what Maher and Tetreault (1994) see as women positioning themselves as both "knowers and learners" (p 129). This positioning of learners as agents in the construction of knowledge raises significant questions, firstly, in relation to the differences between women and then secondly in relation to the place of the experiences of men.

FEMINIST PEDAGOGY AND DIFFERENCE

As issues of difference have come to the forefront in feminist politics a more complex understanding of feminist pedagogy has been developed. The awareness of difference in postionality helped expose received ideas especially dichotomized thinking of 'them' and 'us' on whatever axis 'them' and 'us' is defined. The idea of difference also enabled a deeper understanding of the construction of knowledge to take account of multiple perspectives. Maher and Tetreault (1994) in their ethnographic study of the practice of feminist teachers in a number of different universities in the USA, highlight some of the significant tensions in the development of feminist pedagogy particularly in diverse classrooms. Classrooms today are far more heterogeneous with women and men from a range of class, race and ethnic backgrounds. A simple idea of building a pedagogy and knowledge on the commonality of women's experiences is no longer sufficient. In this study they looked at how "gender and diversity shape teaching, learning and the production of new forms of knowledge" (p 2). For them new forms of diversity offer an opportunity to look at new ways of interaction not just between female teachers and female learners but also between women and men as teachers and as learners in the classroom. New forms of interpretation that explicitly take account of the different positional and cognitive aspects of multiple 'ways of knowing' demonstrate that both men and women use narratives, their emotions, and analytical tools in various ways and in many different voices. (Maher and Tetreault, 1984 p 89).From this Maher and Tetreault develop the idea of 'positional pedagogies':

> In all classrooms positionalities are at work. Teachers and students may assume, aspire to and/or directly challenge and undermine the social structure they inhabit, but they cannot completely step outside them. Yet, if the classroom setting can help students to understand the workings of positional dynamics in their lives, to see them through their 'third eye', then they can begin to challenge them and to create change (p 203).

FEMINIST PEDAGOGY AND CO-EDUCATIONAL SETTINGS

In this chapter we have seen how ideas generated as part of the feminist practice of consciousness raising have significant implications for the educative process. Weiler (1991) points to the difficulties of finding a single coherent definition of feminist pedagogy but in the various writings we do see ideas cohere around the intention of enabling students to work towards social and political change. Much of the discussion about feminist pedagogy is sited within the setting of higher education and so there is the question of whether such practices are equally suitable or applicable to school settings? The dynamics of classroom interaction within school settings has been the subject of a range of studies with empirical data from classroom in a range of national educational systems such as UK, USA, Australia depicting male dominance of classroom space (Howe, 1997). Boys dominate interaction with teachers and seek greater amounts of teacher attention often negatively in the form of reprimand. Further, teachers see boys as more difficult to control and tend to focus on this aspect rather than the engagement of girls. One response to this has been the development of single-gender classrooms within co-educational settings. At one level, this would seem to provide the space for girls to be able to assert themselves and engage in classroom dialogue, in public forums and an opportunity for boys not to be distracted by the girls. This strategy might been seen to avoid rather than challenge existing power dynamics. An alternative response can be found in women's efforts to use feminist pedagogy in co-educational classrooms to challenge efforts to derail a feminist political analysis and to engage all learners.

Whereas CR was in the context of women-only groups, the classroom of an educational institution will be largely co-educational and more than likely increasingly diverse in terms of race and ethnicity. There is the danger of simply perpetuating of patriarchal gender relationships with women once again silenced and their experiences marginalized. As Bell et al. (2000) observe:

> as teachers we must be continually aware of the varieties of student-resistance strategies that we will encounter and be prepared to respond to them in a constructive manner. The paradox of our pedagogy is that we are also providing space for 'master narratives to enter the classroom' (p 40).

Lewis (1990) gives an account of critical episodes in her feminist classroom where there was often resistance or rejection of issues relating to gender and society both from women and men students. She is concerned to develop a form of feminist teaching that enables women to see feminism as offering them the means of creating alternative aspirations. Often in Lewis's experience women students view feminism as a negative discourse that is intended to dismantle what they aspire to in terms of careers or heterosexual relationships rather than providing them with alternative aspirations. She is also concerned that male student's feelings of discomforture are championed by women thus reinforcing their tradition role as care-taker rather than analysed and used to challenge patriarchal relations. Her response to these was to look to the dynamics of the context of the classroom to challenge views that either resist or divert the focus away from exploring the power regimes of gender that underpin social and political spheres as well as structure personal relationships. She argues that:

> the pedagogical implications of such gender relations in the feminist classroom must be taken seriously if we are to understand how and why women students might wish both to appropriate and yet resist feminist theoretical and political positions that aim to uncover the roots of our deeply misogynist culture and give legitimacy to women's desires and dreams of possibility" (p 483).

Constructing issues on simple male/female, oppressor/oppressed dichotomies can lead to conflict, shame, guilt and accusation, none of which are ultimately productive in the project of social and political change. Looking closely at the moments of rejection and resistance has enabled Lewis to develop "an interpretive framework for creating a counter-hegemony from my teaching-practice" (p 487). The analysis and construction of pedagogic practice developed by Lewis centres on the issue of gender relationships in the classroom. A similar approach is advocated by Mills (2000) where there is a respectful but challenging approach adopted with boys to recognise power issues related to patriarchal gender patterns. Mayberry (2000) drawing from hooks (1994) gives an account of a form of feminist pedagogy which invites students to critique the unequal social relations embedded in contemporary society and to ask why these circumstances exist and what one can do about them.

> To achieve these liberatory goals, feminist educators develop and use classroom process skills, many of which are used in collaborative learning environments. Informal relations among class members are built by initiating student-centred experiences such as group activities and group reports. Great care and skill go into developing a learning environment where students work together to design group activities that demonstrate an awareness of the race, class, and gender dynamics that permeate the larger society. Through dialogue and conversation, students and teachers negotiate a curriculum that articulates their needs and concerns. These classroom strategies are designed explicitly to empower students to apply their learning to social action and transformation, recognize their ability to create a more humane social order, and become effective voices of change within the broader social world (p 7).

SUMMARY

Fundamentally CR is an educative process in which women developed not only an understanding of the nature of patriarchal gender relations but political skills and personal skills to support political activism, particularly confidence. The process of CR has also led the way to discussions about identity in learning and in the construction of knowledge. The analysis from CR challenged some of the unquestioned assumptions about the canon of knowledge, the privileging of objectivity and rationality in learning. Further, crucially important in CR was the idea of 'voice' which runs through feminist thinking. The emphasis on women having the space to voice their views, to relate their experiences in secure place pointed up the significance of the political dynamics of learning in an institutional setting. The development of feminist pedagogy has very much been based on this understanding of the sociopolitical dynamics of classroom life. This insight gave rise to a vast range of studies of classroom dynamics across all sectors of education (see Howe 1997 for summary), a pattern which persists (Bell et al., 2001). Though its origins were in the early discussions about the process of CR where the predominant issue was that of the oppression of women, feminist pedagogy has become more nuanced in both practices and theorising around these sets of practices. A set of powerful pedagogies have developed which has helped address, where used, issues of structured inequalities in classroom dynamics. However, these practices very much rely on the role of the teacher in balancing different needs and positions within a classroom. In the next chapter I look at another theme that emerged from discussions about ideologies of gender in feminist utopian texts, that of 'mothering', where teaching has been characterized as mothering.

CHAPTER 6

EDUCATION AS MOTHERING

Introduction

The idea of constructing an alternative society based on principles derived from women's maternal role is a significant theme in feminist utopian thinking. Against a backdrop of war, increased militarisation and ecological disaster, the ideas of nurturing and caring are rich in possibilities for the development of a better society. However, because women's capability to bear children has been used as justification historically to restrict women's roles in the public domain there are also some difficulties. In this chapter, the debates about women's maternal role in feminist utopian thinking and the implications of these for the educative process will be explored.

I will begin by examining the place of the concepts of 'motherhood' and 'mothering' within feminist utopian thinking, mapping out some of the major themes. In this body of work there are three broad constructions of 'the process of mothering: firstly mothering is defined as 'motherhood' based on the biological functions of conception and child birth; secondly, motherhood is defined in terms of child-rearing undertaken by largely women especially during a child's early years and thirdly, mothering rather than motherhood is a caring is a process that can be undertaken by both men and women. The place of motherhood and mothering in the process of social transformation also raises questions about fatherhood and fathering which I will also consider.

When other areas of women's experiences and contributions have been denied or made invisible, women have sought some kind of value in this uniquely female area of activity. In the 1970s, within cultural feminism women's distinctive capacity to bear children became increasingly significant in the formulation of a politics for social transformation. The uniquely female task of being a mother and the values that are associated with the role of mother, the nurturance and care of others could be the founding ideas of a transformed society. In her essay, 'Mother Right' (1997) first published in the early years of Women's Liberation, Jane Alpert links motherhood to the founding of a better society:

> ... feminist culture is based on what is best and strongest in women, and as we begin to define ourselves as women, the qualities coming to the fore are the same ones a mother projects in the best kind of nurturing relationship, to a child (hypertext p 3).

In many feminist utopias, the idea that motherhood as a deeply meaningful and pleasurable role for many women is used as the basis to construct a more just society. Although the possibilities of motherhood and mothering are explored as a means of constructing the basis for a good society are explored in feminist utopian writing the consequences are also appraised critically. Within patriarchal ideologies, femininity and maternity are elided in cultural representations which construct the experience of being a mother as one to which all 'normal' women must aspire because it is the 'natural' function of all adult women. This definition of motherhood helps perpetuate the private/public, nature/culture dichotomies and circumscribes women's lives by directing them to a narrow and less valued set of roles. Many women do not bear children or even undertake the task of child-rearing. However, historically women, because of this capability to bear and give birth, have been barred from or been made invisible within the public domain which has been traditionally regarded as suitable only for men who do not have the 'burden of motherhood'. If motherhood is reduced to the biological function of conception and gestation, this has a deleterious effect on the status and role of women and is the mark of a dystopian society. Ruddick's (1991) in her philosophical exploration argues that maternal thinking should be the basis of a new social order but also opens the possibility that mothering and caring work is something that is both valued and to be shared with men.

MOTHERING AND EDUCATION

In these visions of a eutopia (good or better society) in feminist utopian writing education is constructed as a process of nurturance, which has its origins in the process of mothering. The idea that learning is a natural and relational process and that educational provision should be constructed on the basis of this is not unique to feminism but can be found in discussions particularly about child-centred education. What is distinctive here is that the educative process is constructed as a nurturing relationship mirroring that of mother and child through which an alternative and better society can be established. The educative process comes from the bonding between mother and child, particularly mother and daughter. Taking the idea of women's maternal role and constructing the educative process on this basis has significant implications for the role of women and girls, men and boys as learners as well as educators. The mother and child relationship becomes the prototype ideal of the teacher and learner relationship in which the role of the mother is to form the citizen of the future.

While there are considerable possibilities of looking at mothering and education, there are dangers in constructing the educative role as a 'natural' role for women. Constructing certain roles as natural for women because of their childbearing capabilities distorts both the purpose and practice of education for women and girls as well as limits the role of women and men as educators.

THE HANDMAID'S EDUCATION

Margaret Atwood's (1985) novel *The Handmaid's Tale* provides a graphic illustration of these consequences. Atwood's novel has been criticized for providing an exaggerated and distorted view of gender politics but as she observes:

> ...nothing happens which the human race has not already done at some time in the past, or which it is not doing now, or for which it has not yet developed the technology. We've done it, or we're doing it, or we could start doing it tomorrow. Nothing inconceivable takes place, and the projected trends on which my future society are based are already in motion (Atwood 1985, 85-86).

The 1980s saw the start of the retrenchment and revival of fundamentalist religions, particularly in the USA where fundamentalist Christianity emerges as a political force still very much influential today opposing the demands of feminism for greater equality and the reconstruction of the patriarchal family, what Faludi (1992) terms 'backlash politics'. Margaret Atwood's fictional dystopia was written against the backdrop of this right wing re-assertion of 'traditional values', in particular the values underpinning the male-dominated family structure. A major plank in the justification of the male-headed family is its 'natural', and therefore, moral status. The novel is set in a near future society of Gilead, a theocracy in which women's roles are dictated by their fertility.

In Atwood's dystopia we see how the educative process is shaped by this reductive construction of what it means to be a woman. The education of women is solely in terms of preparing them for their future familial and domestic roles. It might be argued that such a reductive construct has little relevance today when access to education is seen as a human right. However there remains, especially in contexts where girls' and women's access to education is curtailed by cultural, religious or economic considerations, a view that education is either not significant or should largely prepare girls for their future roles as wives and mothers.

In the polluted world of Gilead with a negative replacement birth rate, the conception and bearing of children has become a political imperative which results in severe limitations being placed on women. Women who can conceive and bear children come under strict regulation for the benefit of the powerful in society. This is a rewriting of the Rachel and Leah biblical story in which the handmaid conceives and bears the child of the Commander for his infertile wife. Consequently, the educative process is reduced to preparing the women for this biological task.

The narrator of the novel is able to bear children and so is educated in the Rachel and Leah Re-Education Centre, the "Red Centre". This is an abandoned high school where the regime is a mixture of prison, military training and a convent. The education of fertile women though, is not a nurturing process. It is a strict and demeaning education where harsh punishment ensures compliance. The handmaids are watched over by 'the aunts": "Aunt Sara and Aunt Elizabeth patrolled, they had electric cattle prods slung on thongs from their leather belt" (p 13-14). "Gyn Ed" (p

127) is the main focus where the women are taught about child bearing and childbirth including the ritual for conceiving the Commander's child. The women are not allowed to read or write: the only exception being the Aunts who have this special role in securing young 'virtuous' fertile women.

The educative process is underpinned by ideas of fertility and purity and women, rather than being seen as the victims of male violence, have 'to testify' admitting to past sins:

> But whose fault was it? Aunt Helena says, holding up one plump finger.
>
> Her fault, her fault, her fault, we chant in unison. [...]
>
> Why did God allow such a terrible thing to happen? Teach her a lesson. Teach her a lesson. Teach her a lesson (p 82, italics in the original).

The lesson to be learned is that women's worth is measured in her ability to bear children: "Consider the alternatives," said Aunt Lydia" (p 129) malevolently to the narrator. Infertile women are banished to the toxic regions.

In Atwood's novel we have a very restricted idea of motherhood in which conception and child birth are separated from the process of child rearing. With infertility is now rife, the fertility of young vulnerable women – the handmaids – is now colonised by the powerful. Any child a handmaid bears is given over to the wife of the Commander in order to perpetuate the existing power regimes based on the structure of the patriarchal family of the privileged.

This dystopian vision is critically appraised by the inclusion of alternative possibilities. In the text there are interesting juxtapositions posed by mere glimpses of several different historical moments in the education of the women. As the narrator reflects on her days as a student contemporary readers would recognise this snapshot:

> Moira, sitting on the edge of my bed, legs crossed, ankle on knee, in her purple overalls, one dangly earring, the gold fingernail she wore to be eccentric, a cigarette between her stubby yellow-ended fingers. Let's go for a beer. [...]
>
> In half an hour, I said. I had a paper due the next day. What was it? Psychology, English, Economics. We studied things like that, then. On the floor there were books, open face down, this way and that extravagantly (p 47).

We are aware that not just in the future dystopia of Gilead but women historically have been excluded from academic education. As the narrator walks past an old building she reflects: "Moira once told me that it used to be where the undergraduates ate, in the earlier days of the university. If a woman went in there, they'd throw buns at her" (p 211). There is hope for in the final section of the novel, female academics in a time 250 years hence from Gilead debate the historical significance of the document, 'The Handmaid's Tale' suggesting once again women have access to education. These glimpses here underline the idea that the education of women is very much shaped by the wider sociopolitical construction of what it means to be a woman.

Atwood depicts clearly the severe consequences for women when their role is reduced to the task of child bearing with any education available designed to support this role. However, one of the most poignant aspects of the novel is the handmaid's longing for her own daughter born before the current repressive regime came into being. Motherhood, then, is not simply about the conception and bearing of children but encompasses the task of child rearing which is for many women a deeply important and fulfilling role particularly in the early years of their child's life. In this construction of motherhood, education as mothering takes on a far richer set of meaning and more complex practices.

MAKING PEOPLE

Jessie Bernard in her feminist analysis of motherhood, (1975), argues that motherhood is not solely a biological function but consists of "...customs, traditions, conventions, beliefs, attitudes, mores, rules, laws, precepts and a host of other rational and non-rational norms which deal with the care and rearing of children ... and [has] a powerful symbolic component as well" (p vii). In the eutopian worlds constructed by contemporary feminist writers there is a strong resistance to any reductionist stance in relation to the concept of mother as a biological function, nor is motherhood is simply about caring for individual children, but it is presented as a complex network of cultural practices which has implications for the educative process. A consistent theme running through many pieces of feminist utopian writing is the view that the ethics of nurturing and caring should replace the valorisation of aggression and domination in patriarchal relations.

This theme is exemplified in what Sara Ruddick (1990), calls 'maternal practice' which, she argues, should now be translated from the private sphere of the family into the sphere of public life. Ruddick argues that to be a mother is not simply to give birth. She proposes two types of labour, 'birthing' labour and 'caring' labour, which are not necessarily linked and argues that the latter constitutes motherhood. Being a mother is to take on the responsibility of childcare as a regular and substantial part of one's life. This is what Ruddick characterises as "preservative love" (p 17) which gives rise to a distinctive kind of thinking that of "maternal thinking" (p 28).

If we take Ruddick's construction of mothering as the basis for the educative process, there is a blurring of the line between child rearing and education. Teaching is a nurturing developmental process that is child-centred and based on a relationship between teacher and child akin to that of mother and child. Given the richness of the mother-child relationship and its importance in the child's development in the first years of life, constructing education as a mothering process has a great deal of appeal in promoting the holistic development of well-rounded individual children particularly in a highly accountable and competitive educational environment.

The conflation of mothering and education is explored at length in the feminist utopian classic *Herland* by Charlotte Perkins Gilman (1979). When this novel, first written in serial form during the first wave of feminism in 1915-17, was published in book form in 1979 it found a contemporary audience. The novel is set in the isolated female-only society of Herland which is based on the principle of maternity. Vandyck Jennings, one of three male visitors in Herland in two thousand years, explains:

> You see, they were mothers, not in our sense of hopeless involuntary fecundity, forced to fill and overfill the land, every land, and then see their children suffer, sin and die, fighting horribly with one another; but in the sense of Conscious Makers of People. Mother-love with them was not a brute passion, a mere 'instinct', a wholly personal feeling; it was – a religion (p 68).

A subtle use of irony by Gilman helps contrast different understandings of what it means to be educated. The opening of the novel details the preparations of the three male explorers for the expedition and they are each introduced in terms of their expertise as they make pronouncements about women. These authorative opinions of the 'learned' male characters are juxtaposed with their 'education' during the early days of their visit to Herland so they can understand the basis of this alternative society. Here they have to 'unlearn' their knowledge gained in their own male dominated society but this is a difficult process. When he arrives in Herland and sees this well-ordered and positive society Terry, another of the male visitors, exclaims: "'It's impossible!' [...] 'Women cannot co-operate – it's against nature'" (p 67).The story of the education of the male visitors is told ironically, illustrating some of the misguided assumptions and limitations of not only their own knowledge but also the dominant ideas in their wider society. Though there is a gentle ironic tone in the text we see this educational process as positive, supportive and humane.

Motherhood, that is caring for children, the business of "Making People" (p 69) is the important task fulfilled by a special few in Herland. Somel, one of the women whose task is to guide the male visitors through Herland explains:

> ...child rearing has come to be with us a culture so profoundly studied, practised and with such subtlety and skill, that the more we love our children the less we are willing to trust that process to unskilled hands even our own' (p 83).

In a society based on the principles of maternity, education is a naturalistic process which is concerned with both the physical and intellectual development of children. Somel outlines their theory of education:

> Here is a young human being. The mind is a natural thing as the body, a thing that grows, a thing to use and enjoy. We seek to nourish, to stimulate, to exercise the mind of the child as we do the body. There are the two main divisions in education – you have those of course? – the things it is necessary to know, and the things it is necessary to do (p 104).

The core of the educational process is the development of two powers: "that seem to us basically necessary for all noble life: a clear far-reaching judgement, and a strong well-used will" (p 106). However, education is not simply about children, but about continuing to develop and grow: "When one settles too close in one kind of work there is a tendency to atrophy in the disused portions of the brain. We like to keep on learning, always" (p 105).

Education in Herland is linked intrinsically to the process of social transformation, by improving the population in all aspects with each generation. As Somel explains to Vandyck: "We are at work, slowly and carefully, developing our whole people along these lines. It is glorious work – splendid! To see the thousands of babies improving, showing clearer minds, sweeter dispositions, higher capacities" (p 105-6). It is clear that this is a very positive representation of education as a process of mothering and that its intentions are to ensure the 'good society'. The collapsing of mothering and education here is about re-defining human nature, about making a new people. Lane (1979) in her introduction to *Herland* notes that in Gilman's work: "...education – not formal education but the process by which values permeate an entire social fabric – evolves as a natural device in the creation of a new people, especially the young" (p xxvi).

However, this linking of mothering and education does have a more questionable aspect. "Motherhood is the task of only certain women: Motherhood the highest social service – a sacrament, really; that it is only undertaken once, by the majority of the population; that those held unfit are not allowed even that; and that to be encouraged to bear more than one child is the very highest reward and honour in the power of the state" (p 69). In this Gilman is grappling with some of the discussions about the future of society that were current at the time of her writing this text in 1915. A populist 'utopian' construct is the creation of a super race of humans who, because of their superior traits, are able to live in peace and harmony. These ideas are also found in philosophical and political movements such as Social Darwinism or the Eugenics movement where eugenics was constructed as a progressive solution, the means to bring about improving society. There are serious political, social and moral problems with both positive and negative eugenics. Eugenics was seen to offer the way forward, the selective breeding of 'superior' humans would ensure the continued development of the race and solve particular social problems. In Gilman's vision we are unsure whether it is education or selective breeding that is the means by which the society will be transformed:

> our improvement must be due either to mutation, or solely to education...We certainly have improved. It may be that these higher qualities were latent in the original mother, that careful education is bringing them out, and that our personal differences depend on slight variations in prenatal condition (p78).

Though this discussion in Gilman's novel reflects the contemporaneous debate, the question has a current relevance when we consider the role of the state in ensuring 'fit mothers'. The recent discussion by Tony Blair, the Prime Minister in the UK about 'pre-birth intervention' in relation to the children of vulnerable teenage mothers illustrates the political issues surrounding motherhood (BBC, 2006). This regulation is not only evident within a legal framework but operates at an ideological level as well.

Mothering is a construct shaped by cultural, social and political processes. When added to this conflation of mothering and education, the idea of mothering has significant implications for women and for the educative process. The assumptions underlying education as mothering are based on an idealised construction of mothering but may deny or even pathologies certain practices and attitudes which do not conform to this ideal.

REGULATING MOTHERING

Walkerdine and Lucy's (1988) empirical study, *Democracy in the Kitchen Regulating Mothers and Socialising Daughters* examines the construction of mothering as an educative process especially in the early years before school. The operation of this construction of mothering is vital in shaping education and welfare policies and practices. As Phoenix et al. (1991) remind us: what is widely accepted as 'good mothering' by 'good mothers' is socially constructed and has political implications and social consequences. It is because there are connections between 'the family' and maintenance of the political status quo that official concern is expressed about 'the family' at times when there are changes in family structures (p 25).

Ideas about the importance of the early years in a child's development draw from Bowlby's (1969) work on attachment. Bowlby's work on attachment became central to the role of mothering as well as the development of pre school education. The quality of a child's early social experiences is seen in educational discussions as centrally important, and this, despite the expansion of Pre 5 provision, is predominantly a task undertaken by mothers. There are significant consequences for women as mothers as Walkerdine and Lucey observe "…if you want your child to succeed in the educational system, become a sensitive mother" (p 61). However, the role of a mother undertakes is not simply about nurturing the individual child. There are wider sociopolitical consequences. Walkerdine and Lucey outline a vision of the idealized educative mother – 'the sensitive mother' – forming the citizens of tomorrow:

> The path to democracy begins in the kitchen of the sensitive mother. Here there is supposed to be a nurturing presence that facilitates the development of her child towards natural language and reason. These develop because the sensitive mother is finely tuned to her child's struggle for meaning, extends and elaborates her utterances, transforms her domestic work into play for her child's cognitive development. All these and more are the ways in which so-called natural development is produced. This development, getting at the child through the relay point of the mother, aims to reproduce a reasonable citizen. This citizen imagines herself empowered, autonomous, free. Here, democracy is ensured by the removal from consciousness any sense of oppression, powerlessness, division or exploitation" (p 101).

However, Walkerdine and Lucey are critical of this construction seeing it as a fantasy, an ideal that is, firstly, very class based and secondly, has a significant impact on both mother and children. They re-examined data drawn from an earlier study by Tizard and Hughes (1984) exploring the "...twin histories of oppression, of regulation of mothers in the bourgeois order, which set women against women, rendering one normal and the other pathological, making one responsible for the regulation and oppression of the other" (p 5). Analysing the experiences of women and mothers from working class backgrounds, Walkerdine and Lucey argue that myths about motherhood are deeply oppressive.

There are resonances between Walkerdine and Lucey's discussion and the construction of mothering in Herland. The emphasis on the child's experiences of being mothered as a precursor and a preparation for school has meant that "almost all domestic tasks [are] transformed into pedagogy" (p 22). The nurturing mother who engages the child in everyday tasks, in play is creating the rich learning environment. The expectation that this is part of 'normal' life does have an impact on all women but there is a differential impact relating to social class. For Walkerdine and Lucey, the key question is this: "is the kitchen the place where play and freedom and mother love produce autonomous children, empowered and rational?" (p 30). Walkerdine and Lucey want to reject any validation and pathologising of either the middle-class and working class practices in relation to mothering: they see both as "the object of regulation and oppression but differently" (p 22). The open approach of explanation, encouraging the child to reason and intellectualise is a middle class model of mothering which working class women, because of constraints and pressures, do not use their time in 'play'. This leads to women – frequently working class women – being pathologized as 'bad mothers' but also has consequences for middle class mothers.

Walkerdine and Lucey have two central contentions. Firstly, many working class women do not regulate their daughters in a democratic mode; they make power and conflict visible and painful. For this they are pathologised as 'poor mothers'. Secondly, in a middle class context where women may have the time, power and conflict are not dispersed or eliminated in the democratic kitchen, they are suppressed. Harmony is only on the surface as "beneath reasonableness lies the passions" (p 103). It becomes a matter of the mother's needs versus the child's needs: "women become chained in their homes to suffer the tyrannical rule of their children" (p 104) because this idea of harmony is an illusion. This idealized construction of mothering in which the education of the child is paramount has a significant impact on women leading to a situation where it places women's needs in competition with those of their children. Walkerdine and Lucey looking at the lived experience of women acknowledge that "mothering is clearly both painful and intensely pleasurable" (p 157) and are doubtful of feminist attempts to re-claim motherhood as the basis for sociopolitical change.

THE ROLE OF THE FATHER

Conflating education as mothering raises significant questions about the role of men. In discussions about the educative process there seems to be a very limited consideration of the notion of 'fathering'. Partly this may lie with the conceptual limitations of 'fathering' which in everyday usage refers to the biological act of procreation – to father a child – in contrast to 'mothering' which signals the caring and relational role. However, there are also issues related to the role of the father in patriarchal gender relations. Historically, the role of the father as the breadwinner was a physically distant figure but his position was symbolic both in the constitution of a family and in the distribution of power in patriarchal society. The legal definition of paternity implies both responsibility and ownership and so, traditionally fathers have not only been the breadwinners of the family, but they also have had control over the mothering of their children. As we have seen in Atwood's (1987) novel, the fathering of the child is more important signifying ownership, power and status. In contrast to maternal ideals of caring, nurturing and support, definitions of fatherhood tend to encompass ideas of authority, power and ownership, leaving fatherhood problematic in feminist utopian thinking in the construction of an educative process within a frame of social transformation.

The problematic nature of the idea of 'fatherhood /fathering' as a basis for an sociopolitical order or an educational process is graphically depicted in a feminist utopia, *Swastika Nights* (1938) by Katherine Burdekin, written shortly before the Second World War as a critique of the gender politics evident in Nazism (Koonz, 1988). The society in this fictional utopia is extreme but it, nevertheless, illustrates some of the issues underpinning fatherhood in an unequal society. Women live in camps and their primary function is to produce the next generation of soldiers. They are denied all rights and so complete is their oppression that their only act of resistance is to destroy themselves as a gender and the women have stopped producing daughters who would only be condemned to the same life of total subjugation. In this society women are simply breeders and men as fathers own their male children (daughters are not recognised by their fathers); when a male child is eighteen months old he is handed over to his father in a ritual which denies any bond between the mother and her child: "'Woman where is my son?' 'Here, Lord, here is your son. I, all unworthy have borne'" (p 12). Women are so despised that even being borne by a woman is regarded as something that taints men. What becomes clear from this novel is that such societies based on a hegemonic masculinity have ultimately a deleterious effect on men and women. For men, though their lives might be more tolerable than that of the women, they are oppressed by a militaristic culture that valorises an aggressive form of masculinity which must negates any hint of femininity in a man's behaviour. Any form of education based on this construction of fathering simply perpetuates the power regime.

In a more recent feminist utopian novel, *A Walk to the End of the World* (1974), Suzy McKee Charnas takes up Burdekin's theme of a dystopian society based on the valorisation of masculinity. The founding of a society on such principles has profound consequences for the position of women. This novel is set in a future world devastated by wars and environmental disaster. In Holdfast, women have lost their identity: they are only "unman" (p 5). Women have become simply a brutalised work force or the 'pets' of men and have been reduced to such a subhuman status that they are incapable of using language beyond the most rudimentary patterns of speech. In Charnas's world there is no formal education for girls. Women's position has been so circumscribed that they cannot even act as the first educators to their daughters. There is no sense of mother/daughter bonding, of intergenerational learning. Instead young girls spend the first and formative years of their life 'in the pits', in cages learning what they need to survive in this society. Only the fittest will emerge from the pits who will be able to deal with the hardship experienced by women as a slave labour force and be fit enough to bear strong male children.

In these circumstances, an extreme form of masculinity has been allowed to flourish and this dystopian vision allows us to see significant consequences for constructing an educative process based on a hegemonic form of masculinity. In this society, conflict, competitiveness and violence are integral to any notion of manhood, but the only conflict left is that between father and son because all other enemies have been killed off and women have been reduced to total servitude. Further, the inscription of masculinity with these core attributes disallows any intergenerational exchange whether through family ties or through an educational process. The social role of the father has also been abolished because it has become a dangerous institution. The oedipal drama of male psychosexual development has become institutionalised and the greatest anxiety is a war between the generations. It is believed that inevitably sons will grow to oppose their fathers, so no son knows who his father is: "...old and young are natural enemies; everyone knew that. To know your father's identity would be to feel, however far off, the chill wind of death" (p 24).

Education is not the bonding between the generations as it is in Herland. Instead, boys are at risk from older generations. Education is conducted in the Boy house which "...kept the boys safe and with them their future; here their souls were beaten into a hardness that should be fitting to the soul of men" (p 42). The Boyhouse, resonant of Spartan education, is no haven; instead, education in the Boyhouse is intended to rid the boys of any vestiges of femininity. The regime is harsh and many boys did not survive:

> In discipline is belonging,' the Teacher said. 'In discipline is solidarity among men against the sly evil of the void with which your dams [mothers] have infected you.' And again, 'Discipline is the firm ground on which rugged individualism stands.' And again, 'We are here to melt the fem-fat from your spirits and toughen you into men' (p 109).

Eykar, the main male character, challenges the very foundations of this society by his search for his father: "The man who knew his father's name might do anything, might even make himself immortal with some immense, transfixing gesture" (p 86). But in the meeting between the son and his father there is no challenge to the brutality of this regime by any display of support or affection; instead there is only the exercise of arbitrary male power as Eykar, the son kills his father, Raff Maggomas, and brings about a final apocalyptic conflict.

This text is not simply a version of the oedipal complex but what Charnas' text illustrates so graphically and brutally is the paradox inherent in the construction of masculinity in patriarchal gender relations. Within the construction of gender as bipolar opposites any reshaping of masculinity and fatherhood means it is no longer 'manly' and can only be feminine. These dystopian images in feminist utopian thinking help to spotlight a significant tension in the current debate about the education of boys and the role of men as male educators.

EDUCATION AS FATHERING

In the debates about the education of boys, stimulated by the improved performance of girls over boys in public examinations, has led to a re-consideration of co-education from the perspective of the experience of boys: is there something in the current educational process that is creating barriers to boys' learning and achievement. Included in reasons cited for this are the 'feminised classroom' and the lack of role models for boys. Is there then merit in considering education is terms of 'fathering'?

Mills (2000) raises concerns about some of the simplistic ideas about 'the causes' of boys' underachievement in education. Mills challenges notions that school education is feminised and that the education of boys should be the business of men. He sees this idea that underpins the claims for men's rights and mythopoetic politics as erroneous. The oppression that some men and boys undoubtedly experience because, for example, of poverty, ethnicity or sexuality, has been universalised to make the case that in education all men and boys are discriminated against. The problem, then, is presented as one that is external to men/boys –frequently the result of women's advance in education – rather than problem intrinsically related to the construction of hegemonic masculinities. Hegemonic masculinities have at the core, values such as competitiveness, aggression and violence which perpetuate anti-authority, anti-schools stance that limits boys' engagement in education – what Connell (2000) calls "protest masculinities". For Mills, a more desirable approach would be one that 'respectfully' enables boys and male teachers to explore the way in which boys and males are privileged in the current gender power relationships while, at the same time, create the circumstances for boys' engagement in education. A respectful approach:

> …will recognise the complexities involved in being a boy growing up in a society where particular, often violent masculine qualities are valued over others, and where factors such as class, sexuality, ability/disability, race/ethnicity and age are also implicated in the ways boys come to see the world. However, it will recognise boys' privileged position in gender relations. Thus, such an approach to the education of boys will advocate a politics which goes beyond self-interest and instead encourages boys to act in the interests of social justice (p 236).

Constructing education as fathering is problematic suggesting attitudes and values counter to accepted ideas and practices underpinning but is mothering any less problematic? Mothering, on the other hand, offers some powerful ideas but these might exclude men and boys from the educative process. We, therefore, have to look for a wider understanding of education as 'mothering' that engages boys and men and which challenges hegemonic forms of masculinity that currently act as barriers to learning.

Nancy Chodorow (1978), in her psychoanalytical study of early childhood, *The Reproduction of Mothering,* also argues for the sociopolitical benefits of men becoming involved in childcare roles. Chodorow points to the absence rather than the presence of men especially in child rearing as the root cause of male dominance in society. As a result of men's absence, boys must disrupt their primary identification with their mothers in order to then identify as male. This creates a need in boys for boundaries and autonomy which, to Chodorow's mind, explains the greater aggression in men and their need for power and domination. It is only by involving fathers more in their child's care that the social structure will be reformed. Chodorow's argument demands a reconstruction of fatherhood with men undertaking activities traditionally defined as mothering in order both to alleviate the alienation men suffer in terms of familial and personal caring roles and to create a better social order.

EDUCATION AS CARING

The role of men as educators is a matter of concern as increasingly the gender balance, at all levels of school education at least, is changing significantly. The argument put forward by Mills underlines the view that this issue is not simply a matter of statistics but we need to consider more carefully why male teachers are important as role models and not just for boys, as male educators have a role to play in the learning lives of both girls and boys. If, then, we are to develop the idea of education as 'mothering' we need to consider mothering being widened from a practice that is exclusively a female pursuit.

Marge Piercy's *A Woman on the Edge of Time* (1979) develops the idea that mothering is an activity in which both men and women can participate which then reshapes the wider society as well as the educative process. This novel presents a vision of a future eutopian society of Mattapoisett which is based on small self-sufficient communities. Piercy's draws from Shulamith Firestone's (1971) highly influential radical feminist analysis *The Dialectic of Sex*. Firestone advocates a naturalistic approach to education based on the learner's curiosity and real experiences (which Firestone developed from A.S. Neill, 1962) and non-gendered 'mothering'.

Thus in Mattapoisett the children's house is one designed to enable the children to explore, experiment, determine their own learning.

> Wandering through the rooms, she found some low ceilinged, some opening into fisheye windows, into greenhouses and porches. Some rooms crept into nooks and crannied, small staircases. Others led them to courts full of plants, delicate apparatus, sundials and water clocks, star maps and telescopes. A fountain gurgled. In it three naked children waded with a curly puppy. Birds hopped in the vines, carp lazed in the small stream that flowed through a room whirring with machines into a courtyard, where a construction project was going on with children of seven or eight wielding miniature hammers, planes, and saws (p 133).

Learning is also something that is seen as a lifetime pursuit and something to be structured into the organisation of the community. All adults have a sabbatical every seven years to go away and learn something they wish where this is study, learn a new skill or write. When Connie, the visitor from contemporary society, witnesses a group of children working outside she questions what we mean by learning:

> …she said, 'but they can't possibly learn as much that way as they would in a classroom with a book!' 'They can read. We all read by four or so,' Jackrabbit said. 'But who wants to grow up with a head full of facts always working, always studying. We think, what person thinks person knows has to be tried out all the time. Placed against what people need. We care a lot *how* things are done' (p 131, italics in the original).

Women in this society have given up their capacity to bear children in order to produce a more equal society. The uniquely female capability of bearing a child is replaced by a machine which allows both men and women to have a pivotal role in the nurturing of young children. Men who want to become one of the three co-mothers of a child take female hormones to be able to lactate and feed the child. This sharing of women's 'power' is fraught with dilemmas; Piercy's – at the time notorious – image of the bearded male mother breast feeding a baby, might be read as a dystopian image with men colonising what was once a uniquely female area. However, by radicalising the structure of the family, and reconstructing the roles of men and women in the care and nurturance of children and young people, the people of Mattapoisett have been able to create an educative process which is not gendered – in the sense that both women and men play an equal role. Further, education is affirming of intergenerational bonds.

> We believe old people and children are kin. There's more space at both ends of life. That closeness to birth and to death makes a common concern with big questions and basic patterns. We think old people, because of their distance from the problems of growing up, hold more patience and can be quieter to hear what children want. Not everyone who teaches is old – we all teach. The kids work with us. We try to share what we have learned and what we don't know…I think maybe growing up is less mysterious with us since the adult world isn't separate (p 132).

Education as mothering has become imbued with ideas of caring that are not gendered and this makes demands on both women and men. Piercy's utopian vision helps us to appreciate the significance of this step:

> It was part of women's long revolution. When we were breaking all the old hierarchies. Finally there was one thing we had to give up too, the only power we ever had, in return no more power for anyone. Because as long as we were biologically enchained, we'd never be equal. And males would never be humanized as loving and tender. So we all became mothers (p 115).

EDUCATION AND CARING

Feminist utopian discussions about mothering and education are not confined to fictional works but are also the subject of philosophical consideration. Nel Noddings in several of her works (for example, 1984, 1988, 2002) provides a vision of the educative process based upon the ethic of caring which in turn is based on that of the mother and child. Noddings argues that: "The mother's voice has been silent. Human caring and the memory of caring and being cared for...for the foundation of ethical response" (1984 p 1).Noddings puts forward an alternative ethics, one not based on 'law and principle' (p 2) but one instead based on a feminine viewpoint: she accepts that this does not mean all women behave like this and that men too are capable of behaving in this caring way. She sees this viewpoint as "...feminine in the deep classical sense" (p 2) in which ethical behaviour stems from human affective response. Noddings identifies two key concepts 'one-caring' and 'cared-for' and the caring relationship is between the one-caring and the cared-for. Centrally important in this construction is that the human affective response is the core of the human condition. We act morally to ensure the caring relationship. Noddings argues that "the one-caring has one aim: to preserve and enhance caring in herself and in those with whom she comes into contact" (p 174).

The core of the educative process is the nurturing of the ethical ideal to sustain our mutual dependence. Noddings rejects the idea that the core of consciousness is anguish but instead is "...joy as a basic human affect" (p 6). Caring is related to growth and self-actualisation of the other person. The caring relationship is something that is a skill acquired through practice, dialogue and learning to be able to attribute the best possible motive to incidents or actions that are not ethical. Caring is the first aim of both parenting and of education and any aspect of education should, therefore, be viewed in this light. Further:

> The primary aim of every educational institution and of every educational effort must be the maintenance and enhancement of caring. Parents, policy, social workers, teachers, preachers, neighbours, coaches and other siblings must all embrace their primary aim. It functions as end means and criterion for judging suggested means. It established the climate, the first approximation to the range of acceptable practices, and a lens through which all practices and possible practices are examined (p 173).

Noddings rejects any attempts to divide parenting and teaching where traditionally parenting is the area where caring is developed. She rejects the idea that schools train intelligence and home and church train morality and emotional well-being. Instead caring is something that is developed and evident across all institutions and arenas: it is " a community-wide response" (p 171). Caring, then, is central to education; it is both the goal of education and the means through which people are educated. This idea of caring shapes the role of the teacher which is centred on a special caring relation – "first and foremost 'one-caring' in which she meets the student directly but not equally" (p 175). Noddings defines the teacher as: "the one-caring" (p 178). This shapes her purpose and actions – acting as one-caring is also modelling one-caring: "By conducting education morally, the teacher hopes to induce an enhanced moral sense in the student" (p 179). Noddings argues for the importance of the 'cared-for', that is the student in the process. She cites schools where there is physical and verbal abuse and argues that by establishing caring there will be both one-caring teachers and a sense of the cared-for student who contributes to the relationship through "... a responsiveness that completes the caring" (p 181).

This approach to ethics as caring is feminine in Nodding's view. It is important to recognise that gendered nature of this vision in that Noddings views the approach to ethics as caring is feminine: "our ethic of caring springs from woman's conception of their ethical self as one-caring" (p 182). This is the central idea underpinning Nodding's argument and the prototype is the mother and child relationship and in education we must guard against: "...the excessive efforts at abstraction, objectivity and detachment in our schools which are a manifestation of the father's psychological need to take possession of the child" (p 182).

There are many attractions to constructing education as a mothering process particularly it shapes an idea of education as a process of human growth and formation, of holistic development rather than a narrowing of schooling on the acquisition of skills, knowledge and competences: it helps to centre the person. However, I discussed earlier, does this idea run the risk of alienating men and boys? We have difficulty shaping an equivalent ideal in terms of fathering because of the cultural inscription of that term. Nevertheless, the problematic of fatherhood is a critical issue to engage with when considering education as caring and so we need to explore the possibilities and issues related to the reconstruction of fatherhood.

Burgess (1997) in exploring images of fatherhood and identifies some of the challenges in this, particularly where some neo-right movements seem to be attempting to reclaim fatherhood in terms of asserting male dominance of the family. These attempts to reassert fatherhood seem to be an attack on women's position both in the family and in the public domain: such claims to the rights of fathers seem to retrench women's subordinate role as natural. Burgess argues that part of the difficulty has been the idealization of motherhood:

> The more idealised mothers have become, the more it has been necessary to 'split off' negative perceptions about them and put them somewhere else. The natural repository has been fatherhood, which has long been perceived as motherhood's polar opposite (p 21).

We have seen this clearly in the dystopian images in feminist utopian writing highlighting the problematic nature of the concept of 'fatherhood' in patriarchal gender relation.

Doherty (1997) argues that we have not yet evolved "a set of powerful cultural norms for how to be a good father outside the committed partnership with the mother and outside the unique breadwinner role with live-in children" (p 225) but I would argue that we have to go further than this structural issue and look to the definition of fathering in terms of the ethic of caring identified by Noddings. We have to acknowledge that "For men to become close to their children, these will have to be taken as seriously and tackled as consciously as the dismantling of barriers to women's participation in the wider world" (Burgess, 1997, p31). Reconstructing fatherhood seems to be one of the challenges. However, is this simply about bringing fatherhood and motherhood together: "if there are those who worry about this change, who see it as part of an androgynous drift that renders fatherhood culturally superfluous, there are more, I think, who see this mode of generative fathering as a positive development that opens up new possibilities for father-child connections" (Griswold, 1997, p 85). Hawkins and Dollahite (1997) build on Erikson's (1964) work on generativity, that is caring for the next generation: "fathering that meets the needs of the next generation across time and context (pxiii)".

Constructing teaching as mothering has many attractive qualities but we need to explore how this idea and sets of practices it permits, valorises both women and men as educators as argued by Nel Noddings (2002):

> The new education I envision puts a high value on the traditional occupations of women. Care for children, the aged, and the ill must be shared by all capable adults, not just women, and everyone should understand that these activities bring special rewards as well as burdens (p 95).

This vision of education as caring would have a significant impact on the structures and practice of education for example, smaller schools, removal of age segregation. However, it also will influence the role of parents and with a realignment of parents and teaching. Noddings is advocating a feminine approach to education which will require a change in the structure of schools, a move away from the bureaucratic structures and hierarchies based on "the traditional masculine structure" (p 200). There is a move towards "de-professionalizing education" (p 197) in order to develop the spirit of caring which also can be defined as "maternal attitude" (p 197). Noddings also constructs the curriculum as gendered arguing that the current constructions of the school curriculum is a masculine project (p 192) which is centred on standards and the maintenance of these which has the effect of " the systematic de-humanization of both female and male children through the loss of the feminine" (p 192-3). Instead, she proposes an alternative woman-centred approach:

> Women by our very nature, are unlikely to seek domination in education; our circles will be circles of support and not of power. But it is time for the voice of the mother to be heard in education (p 200).

The idea of education as mothering in these terms raises challenge about how we determine curricula as well as pedagogic practice. As part of the feminist project of sociopolitical change, these aspects of education have come under considerable scrutiny. We turn to these issues in the next chapter.

SUMMARY

In this chapter I have explored the conflation of mothering and education and have examined the possibilities of this by exploring feminist utopian visions of sociopolitical order based on different constructions of motherhood and mothering. As its core as eutopian concept, education as mothering allows us to envision the educative process as a relational process centering on human growth and development. Whether we conceive of education as mothering or mothering as education, we need to recognise there are significant consequences for both women and men. As the teaching profession globally becomes increasing dominated by women in all sectors of the profession, indicating perhaps that this is not seen as an attractive profession for men, we should be cautious of creating further barriers by creating a cultural inscription that excludes them. Nevertheless if we are seeking sociopolitical changes to create the good society we should not retreat from a position which reifies values and practices that are about care and nurture. Perhaps the task is one not of excluding men but of redefining their role in the family, in social agencies such as caring and educational professions based on values of care and nurturance especially intergenerational roles of parent and teacher.

In this chapter I have drawn from feminine inscribed contexts – both fictional and material – to shape ideas about what it means to educate for the good society. In the next chapter we look at another domain which is becoming increasingly significant in education and one which historically has been a masculine-inscribed arena of endeavour, that of technology particularly digital technologies and the development of virtual reality.

CHAPTER 7

CYBERFEMINIST VISIONS

Introduction

In an increasingly technologised society, many areas of life are now mediated by particularly digital technology including economic, education, social and cultural activities. Digital technology is a term covering a wide variety of information and communication technologies particularly the internet which provides not only instant access to leisure and commercial activities, to knowledge but also to a 'virtual reality'. This increasing insertion of technology into human culture is a matter of intense debate in feminism whether such developments could lead to a utopian context where women no longer occupy a subordinate position or even a genderless world or whether these developments will reinforce patriarchal regimes of power and increase the control of women. These digital technologies are having a significant impact on the educative process itself, with these technologies reshaping what we understand as the roles of learner and teacher, of schools and indeed, what it means to be educated. This development of digital technologies could also have profound consequences for the issue of gender in education.

Within education, a critical question is whether the digital technologies could help remove the significance of gender or whether there is the risk that the traditional male inscription of technology will lead to women and girls once again being marginalized both within the wider society and within education. In this chapter I will explore the wider debates feminist utopian thinking about technology and gender to consider some of the issues in relation to the gender and education in a context of an increasing use of technology in learning and pedagogy. What are the issues related to the intensive use of digital technologies for both women and men as educators and as learners? Do the digital technologies hold the promise of an educative process in which gender is no longer significant? I will, firstly, explore debates in feminist utopian writings concerning gender and technology, particularly focusing digital technologies, and then consider the possibility of technology supporting the development of a sociopolitical order where gender no longer has a social significance.

WOMEN AND TECHNOLOGY

Within feminist thinking and politics, technology occupies a problematic position being seen, on the one hand, as a means of promoting greater gender equality and, on the other hand, the means of intensifying the subordination of women. In a number of the other feminist utopian novels we have explored such as *The Wanderground* (Gearhart, 1979) and *A Walk to the End of the World* (Charnas, 1989) dystopian societies are portrayed as the outcome of 'man's' drive for an increasingly technologically dependent economy and culture. In Piercy's (1979) utopian novel, *A Woman on the Edge of Time* the good society was a return to a low-tech pastoral society. However, despite the seeming pastoral nature of this society, the eutopian quality of Mattapoisett is attributable to the use of technology: reproductive technologies which helped to dismantle patriarchal gender relations and the use of technology based weaponry to preserve this society from outside invasion. There is then great ambivalence towards technology in feminist utopian thinking. Clearly 'technology' is a very wide term but within feminist thinking debates have been concerned largely with technology in three broad areas: reproductive technologies (for example, Arditti et al., 1989) technology and war (for example Cook and Kirk, Ruddick, 1990) and digital technologies (Plant 1998, Hawthorne and Klein, 1999).

Early discussions in second wave feminism were predominantly focused on reproductive technologies whether these hold the potential of women's liberation or are the source of an intensification of control of women. Firestone's (1971) early feminist utopian text, *The Dialectic of Sex*, is one of the few radical feminist texts in second wave feminism where there is a wholehearted endorsement of the potential of reproductive technologies to liberate women. As the women's peace movement developed in the 1980s and 1990s technological development became aligned with militarisation and weaponry so considerable unease arose about the increased use of technology. Attempts to extend the range and use of reproductive technologies were seen as an invasion of women's unique role and power. The argument put forward by Arditti et al (1989) is typical. "The new reproductive technologies offer the possibility of controlling the lives of women at a level previously unheard of through patriarchal support, control and regulation of the technologies. New methods for genetic screening of embryos, sex-predetermination and sex-selection are constantly being refined and developed further, whilst research into causes and the prevention of infertility remains a low priority in the scientific and medical world" (p xv). Debates concerning the use of technology – whether in terms of the environmental impact, military expansion or in terms of women's reproductive capabilities – still continue. However, as digital technologies have become more pervasive in everyday life, there has been increased attention on this particular area of technology within feminist utopian thinking. Whereas previously technology was seen as destructive of the good society, the growth of digital technologies has produced a more ambivalent response within feminist utopian thinking and we can see competing positions emerging in cyberfeminist utopian writings

ENGAGING WITH TECHNOLOGY

There are more engaged discussions of gender and technology in the works of a number of feminist writers particularly Donna Haraway and Sadie Plant whose ideas have contributed to the development of thinking within 'cyberfeminism'. Most discussions of cyberfeminism go back to Donna Haraway's (1990) text *A*

Manifesto for Cyborgs in which she poses the figure of the cyborg as disruptive of patriarchal bi-polar construction of gender. Haraway's essay is an important feminist utopian text because it takes the question of gender politics forward into an era of rapid technological change which is radically affecting the material lives of women. Since the publication of this essay in 1985, there have been significant debates about digital technologies and gender in which texts as diverse as Judith Butler's (1990, 1993) theoretical discussions of gender(explored in chapter four) and Sadie Plant's (1998) speculative text, *Zeros and Ones*. Some of these ideas are also taken up in Piercy's third fictional utopia *A Body of Glass* where cyborgs and cybernectically enhanced humans have been created to counter the influence of transnational corporations in a globalised economy. Feminist cyberpunk utopias such as Melissa Scott's (1994) *Trouble and her Friends* are also sources where issues related to women and digital technologies are explored. These feminist utopian writers have all raised issues pertinent to a consideration of gender and the digital technologies. The critical question for feminist writers has been whether digital technologies particularly cyberspace, allow women to play with gendered identities or whether we should be concerned that technology is perpetuating and reproducing patriarchal gender regimes of power?

In these discussions about gender and digital technologies there are recurring concerns that have significant implications for gender and education. For Dale Spender (1995) in her book, *Nattering on the Net*, the main issue is access for women both in terms of having opportunities to use hardware and also to enter the virtual space. It is only by full engagement that women and girls will be able to use what are powerful medias for learning. However, these technologies are not only dominated by men but are being used to reproduce hegemonic forms of masculine behaviours that alienate women and work to exclude them from these powerful medias for learning. Given this male-inscription of digital technology another recurring theme in cyberfeminist writings is the task of transforming the socio-cultural context of digital technologies so women can participate in the educative and economic opportunities these technologies offer. Sadie Plant (1996) seeks to open up this possibility of changing the cultural inscription by looking at women's roles historically and currently in technology. Plant, though, should not be seen as advocating the creation of a completely separate female virtual world. Instead highlights the disruptive potential of cyberspace offering the possibility of a more playful approach to gender. In this discussion, Plant takes up ideas from Donna Haraway's (1990, 1997) work.

Although Haraway's (1990) *A Manifesto for Cyborg* is a relatively early text, it remains a key work in feminist utopian thinking exploring not only the position of women and technology but she uses this to consider the development of a politics and strategy to bring about social and political change. Haraway takes issue with the dominant women-centred ideologies within feminism in the mid-1980s, challenging the idea that women, because of a shared biology or shared experiences of oppression, will 'naturally' come together in political action to bring about a more equal society. Part of the impact of Haraway's essay has been her suggestive use of the 'cyborg' as a liberatory figure for women. This use of the cyborg points to the possibilities of digital technologies disrupting ideas of gender being natural and determined and the basis for the sociopolitical order by challenging hegemonic ideologies that position bi-polar gender as a natural and determined basis for a sociopolitical order, whether it is a male or female dominated society.

BOYS' TOYS?

Dale Spender (1996) sees great potential in the impact of digital technologies on the process of learning offering powerful and effective alternatives to learning than the traditional didactic modes of knowledge transmission. However, there is the danger that women and girls will become excluded from this area. After an initial flurry of women enrolling onto computing courses in universities, this subject has become a male dominated which has wide reaching consequences in terms of achievement. The exclusion of women and girls from digital technologies will limit their ability to progress in education.

Spender points to a circularity in the argument about gender and computing which compounds the exclusion of girls: boys have more to do with computers and so acquire interest and competence and as they have more interest and competence they have more opportunity to develop their skills. Further women and girls are marginalized through typical male behaviour. Spender reveals how the same rules of mixed sexed interaction apply with men consistently dominating, marginalizing women who try to engage and when women participation rises, men complain bitterly: "women have fewer rights to discourse in cyberspace and the penalties for challenging male control could be even harsher than in real life" (p 195). Spender describes physical and verbal strategies boys use to restrict girls access to computers, a phenomenon observed across all sectors of education from early years to HE: "It's the masculine relationship to the machine which seems to bring out the worst in some men" (p 183). This same pattern of exclusion is evident on the internet.

Partly because men far out number women and partly because of the anonymity the Internet offers: "the discourse is male, the style adversial. The premises are winning and losing" (p 198). Spender catalogues the intimidation and threat to women online and sees this not as the behaviour of a small number of men but instead the systematic means of threatening and excluding women: "sexual harassment is becoming the modus operandi of the new world; the medium of communication for the generation of wealth and the support of power" (p 210). Thus the issue is not just about access to the hardware of digital technologies but is also a question of the cultural underpinnings of cyberspace which, as it is currently constructed, is alien to women and girls. Spender argues that there are sets of values and ideas that women and girls do not want to buy into this "anarchy of cyberspace" (p 174). Even women involved in computing see this as a masculine space standing for values they reject. It would be tempting to argue for the creation of a separate virtual space for women. However, ultimately such spaces do not challenge the dominant values of cyberspace. Camp (1996), writing of 'Systers' a women's discussion space, argues that "the very strength that Systers offers can make it a sanctuary" but this limits women's potential and so it "is important to go back out into the public debate and remain visible" (p 121). Increasingly cyberspace is one of the means of understanding the world and so women must be part of its development. It is around issues related to women and digital technologies that cyberfeminism has developed.

CYBERFEMINISM

The term 'cyberfeminism' is variously attributed to the VNS Matrix (1991), an Australian group of multimedia artists who produced a manifesto to lay out their purposes in their artistic endeavours, and to Sadie Plant (1996) in her speculative work *Zeros + Ones*. The term is now used to define the debates and activities of feminists dealing with the context and issues raised by the use of technologies, especially the digital technologies. As Wilding (1997) notes there has been a resistance to defining the term 'cyberfeminism' in anything but the broadest of terms. Hawthorne and Klein (1999), for example, see cyberfeminism as:

> a philosophy which acknowledges, firstly, that there are differences in power between women and men specifically in the digital discourse; and secondly that CyberFeminists want to change that situation...Cyberfeminism is political, it is not an excuse for inaction in the real world, and it is inclusive and respectful of the many cultures which women inhabit (p 2).

Cyberfeminism, in a body of work both aesthetic and political activities, looks to the development of a feminist theory and politics in and about the expanding digital technologies. Faith Wilding and the Critical Art Ensemble (1998b) regard cyberfeminism as "a promising new wave of feminist thinking and practice" (p 1) in which cyberfeminism is "questioning, theorizing and actively confronting" (p 1) not only cyberspace but the hardware and software that supports the virtual reality of the internet. The digital technologies, particularly the internet have also, argue Hawthorne and Klein (1999), the potential "to consciously subvert the dominant knowledge system" but they add an important caveat which underlines the view that it is essential that women are fully engaged in this arena: "it involves knowing that knowledge and being able to participate in it" (p 8). The digital technologies provide the means to promote three aspects vital in the development of feminist politics: connectivity, critique and creativity.

The new technologies have a huge potential for social and political development: "cyberspace has the potential to be egalitarian, to bring everyone into a network arrangement. It has the capacity to create community; to provide untold opportunities for communication, exchange, and keeping in touch" (Spender 1995, p 229). In an era of social and political fragmentation, women connecting virtually through the internet can once again become the political force that collective action had in the early years of Women's Liberation Movement. The power of digital technologies can be utilised as a tool to promote social change but at the same it is important to recognise the power of these technologies to reinforce existing power relations. Consequently, the issue is not one solely of women's access to digital technologies. A critical awareness of the sociopolitical workings within cyberspace is equally important: "[t]he technology and technological processes to which women currently have access [such as emails and computers] are the consequence of structural economic necessity" (Wilding et al. 1997, hypertext). So included in this educational process should be the development of a critical capacity that exposes the use of technology to perpetuate the oppression of women. Thus,

> Cyberfeminism could provide a consciousness raising site where women can tell stories about their experiences with all the different aspects of technology, and how it affects their lives. Such a site could teach women to question the increasing transparency of technological incursion into their workplaces and into everyday life (Wilding et al. 1997, online text).

Cyberspace offers the potential not just to comment on the existing regimes of power but the possibility of constructing alternative sociopolitical orders. Creativity, the third area highlighted by Hawthorne and Klein (1999), offers further strategies for the use of digital technologies to seek change in gender relations. As a new arena, women have the opportunity to shape the developing electronic culture through their own artistic endeavours. Digital technologies not only the means to connect rapidly on a global scale but they provide new forms of writing particularly hypertext and the facility to create multimedia productions which can be utilized to challenge the inscription of cyberspace with hegemonic ideologies of masculinity and instead develop a female oriented cyberculture. Thus Braidotti (1996) argues that:

> The most effective strategy remains for women to use technology in order to disengage our collective imagination from the phallus and its accessory values: money, exclusion and domination, nationalism, iconic femininity and systematic violence (hypertext).

One of the early expressions of cyberfeminism was from a group of artists, the VNS Matrix who draw from previous activism of 'cunt art' to produce their own manifesto for artistic practice in an electronic environment. The intention to challenge patriarchal gender regimes is clear:

> ...we believe in joussance madness holiness and poetry/we are the virus of the new world disorder/rupturing the symbolic from within/saboteurs of big daddy mainframe...infiltrating disrupting disseminating corrupting the discourse/we are the future cunt (hypertext)

Cyberfeminism is still very much evolving and these ambitions have yet to be realized. Challenging the dominant power regimes through artistic endeavour is one form of activism. An alternative approach is found in Sadie Plant's speculative work where she seeks to recover technology as an arena where women have actively participated not just as consumers or users of technology but as creators.

DEFINING ZERO

Dale Spender advocates for women's active engagement in digital technologies to exploit the potential of this area for social and political change. However, for the majority of women there seems little promise of such change. Women's role in the uniform and repetitive routines to maintain bureaucracies seem to place women in a subordinate role as simply as operators of technology rather than as a creator. As the digital world expands, women are involved in the use of technology through their occupational and domestic roles but these are essentially operational roles. Further, it is mainly women who work in large assembly factories in the microprocessing industries owned by transnational corporations – these women are the "virtual aliens" (Plant 1996, p 74). Indeed, Ruis (1999) sees the use of technology as intensifying rather than liberating women: "[t]he mechanism of cyberspace, its fluency and time-space compression, mirrors the transnational models of capital accumulation offering illusions of democracy, opportunity and agency for some" (p 25). Further as Escobar (1999) argues that the potential of cyberspace is not available to the vast majority of women but instead only "to the networked elites the world, culturally connected by new lifestyles and spatially secluded in expensive enclave communities" (p 25). Similarly, Plant argues that in the western world technology is not neutral but technology becomes tools to be used in ways determined by and to the advantage of those who make and use them.

> The user and the used are merely perceptible elements, the identifiable components which are thrown up by – and serve also to contain – far more complex processes. The weaver and the loom, the surfer and the Net: none of them are anything without the engineerings which they both capture and perpetuate (Plant 1996, p 77).

Women need to become active participants and creators in cyberspace. Plant seeks to reclaim technology for women through a mythic vision of women and technology which she creates by building up a mosaic of women's engagement in technology drawing from history and legend and so exposes what has been hidden by the inscription of technology as male in western culture. Among these pieces of women's history Plant looks to legend and explores the way in which Amazon women used technology to make the weapons necessary to sustain their way of life. Further, she makes an analogy between weaving and the development of software. In weaving women's imagination of evident in the design, shape and pattern of fabric and these are 'hidden messages' of women's agency, similar to workings of the microprocessing behind the computer screen. Plant also draws on historical examples of women's substantial contribution to the development of digital technology, for example, the work of Ada Lovelace, an 18th century mathematician or the women involved in the development of a decoding machine, the forerunner of modern computers, at the Betchley Park intelligence operation in Great Britain during World War II. Such contributions by women have been seen as either derivative or of minor interest. This is clearly the case with Lovelace whose work is seen merely an appendix to the work of Louis Menabrea, an Italian military engineer. However, Lovelace's work is an extended exploration of the creation of a "difference machine' a machine capable of undertaking calculations, like an early 'computer'.

Plant sees the new digital technologies alongside other technologies as contributing to the blurring of gender boundaries but the power regimes work to constantly reinforce these boundaries. The construction of virtual reality particularly is reified as a male inscribed arena: "this Phallic quest has always played a major role in the development and popularization of visual techniques" (p 181). Here, though Plant is not content to argue for a female oriented virtual space but the task is to exploit the disruptive potential of digital technologies particularly cyberspace to develop more fluid understandings of what it means to be human:

> the digital revolution has spawned a vast swathe of debate about cyborgs, replicants, and other posthuman, inhuman, extrahuman entities which are complicating orthodox Western notions of what it is to be a human being to be human being. ... This new malleability is everywhere: the switches of transsexualism, the perforations of tattoos and piercings, the indelible markings of brands and scars, the emergence of neural and viral networks, bacterial life, prostheses, neural jacks, vast numbers of wandering matrices (p 177).

Within patriarchal ideologies being human is a deeply gendered concept. The question now is whether cybertechnologies, as both Haraway and Plant suggest, can disrupt patriarchal ideologies of gender.

BINARY GENDER

The view that women have been placed as the second sex occupying a subordinate position in patriarchy has been a pivotal idea within the development of feminist politics. It is worth recalling that historically sex/gender have not always been perceived as bipolar. Historically, the female body did not have the status of being a distinct sex. Laqueur (1990), in his analysis of the construction of the body prior to the nineteenth century, argues that a one-sex model held that a woman's body was a variation of the prototype male body rather than a different sex.

Irigaray plays with this notion in her essay 'This sex which is not one' (1985) in which she argues that women are not the second sex as De Beauvoir (1977) proposed, indeed women are not even a distinct sex because we are invisible in the sex economy of patriarchy. Within Irigaray's utopian writings a significant theme is the transformation our understanding of the notion of 'woman' as the basis for the development of a new and better society. Irigaray argues that to define the notion of 'woman' is not possible within the language of patriarchy. The foundational ideas of patriarchy are based on a 'hom(m)osexual economy': "The law that orders our society is the exclusive valorisation of men's needs/desires, of exchange among men" (1985b p 170). The differences between the sexes are not symbolised or represented within patriarchal discourse, 'woman' is seen to have no self-defining features: she is simply perceived as lack or absence. The female body has always been represented in male discourse as a defective male; now women should reclaim their bodies in order to constitute the subjectivity they are denied in patriarchal discourse: "...the female body is not to remain the object of men's discourse or their various arts but that it becomes the object of female subjectivity experiencing and identifying itself..." (1993 p 59). Plant picks up this theme in her exploration of women and technology by drawing an analogy between the patriarchal construction of sex and the binary machine code in computers, the zeros and ones:

> It takes two to make a binary, but all these pairs are two of a kind, and the kind is always kind of one. 1 and 0 make another 1. Male and female add up to man. There is no female equivalent. No universal woman at his side... (p 35).

She challenges the notion of zero as 'nothing'. She looks to the origins of zero in order to put forward an alternative meaning.

> Zero was always something very different from the sign which has emerged from the West's inability to deal with anything which, like zero, is neither something in particular nor nothing at all. And it is certainly the case that, with or without the signs that represent them as inert negativities, holes themselves are never simply absences of positive things...Adrift in the doped lattices of a silicon crystal, a hole is a positive particle before it is the absence of a negatively charged electron, and the movement of electrons toward the positive terminal is also a flow of holes streaming back the other way. Holes are charged particles running in reverse. For the quantum physicist, 'holes are not the absence of particles but particles travelling (sic) faster than the speed of light' (p 57).

In this Plant is attempting to reconstruct what it means to be a woman. But such definitions maintain gender difference. One of the perennial tensions in feminism is whether we should regard women's physical difference from men as a weapon used in the perpetuation of our oppression or as a tool to bring about our liberation. The body has been a significant issue in feminist thought, in particular, challenging Cartesian dualism which separates the mind and body within patriarchal discourses. This dualism is gendered with male conflated with the mind and female the body which has a profound impact on women's position within patriarchal society. The conflation of female/body in patriarchal discourses has meant that for women developing a politics of gender, the body is double edged because it is the physical make up of the body that mark women as different from men.

The female body is problematic in patriarchal discourses, being simultaneously an object of desire and repudiation, of worship and fear. What constitutes being a woman is heavily determined by an idealised femininity, the construct of the 'Eternal Female' which is used to control women. The disruptive qualities of women whose bodies do not conform to the idealised image of feminine beauty have been reclaimed within feminist thinking as figures of empowerment (Russo, 1988). However, this reclaiming perpetuates rather than challenges patriarchal power relationships based on a bipolar construction of gender.

In the speculative discussions by feminist writers about cyberspace, the blurring of the boundaries between human and machine is used to realise greater plurality and slipperiness in our understandings of gender. In cyberspace, Plant (1996) argues that "no one is or has one sex at a time, but teems with sexes and sexualities too fluid and volatile and numerous to count" (p 212). The disruptive potential of cyberspace is an attractive idea seeming to suggest the possibility of a utopian space where gender is no longer significant. However, considerable issues are raised by this.

BODY/FEMALE AND MIND/MALE

In cyberspace there is the merging of organic and machine and for Melissa Scott (1994) in her feminist cyberpunk novel, *Trouble and Her Friends*, cyberspace has become a site of struggle and resistance. She draws on the coalitional strategies of queer politics to construct this alternative community which exists both materially and virtually. The community of gay and lesbian crackers stand in opposition to the increasing corporate and governmental control of cyberspace. In cyberspace Trouble and her cracker friends go by alternative identities in order to crack secure domains of government and big business often for other big businesses. Through 'brain worms' these crackers can use all their senses in cyberspace to seek out the information:

> they can see, taste, smell and touch this data as they walk through the virtual world of the nets .On the net itself, of course, things are different. Once you plugged yourself into the system – either via the implanted dollies-box and dollies-slot, the direct-on-line-image processor system, which gave a text-speech-and-symbol interface, or through the full-sense brainwork, with it molecular wires running directly into the brain that let you experience virtuality as though it was real – it was easy enough to find your way around the nets (p 14).

It is this linking of body and machine in cyberspace in which corporeal experiences are replaced by purely cerebral experiences, where the line between human and machine is blurred that ideas of gender are also disrupted. Cyberspace is a secret, dangerous but deeply seductive world where an individual can play with gender.

Such playfulness can help to disrupt patriarchal ideas of gender. However Sunden (2001), argue that cyberpunk tends to emphasize rather than challenge the Cartesian mind/body dichotomy. The image of the body as 'meat' goes back to William Gibson's (1995) *Neuromancer*, published in 1984 and regarded as the first cyberpunk novel. This image now pervades cyberpunk writings potentially reinforcing the patriarchal male/mind and female/body dichotomy. Nixon (1999) takes this view and argues that cyberpunk as represented by Gibson and other male writers "creates an alternative, attractive, but hallucinatory world which allows not only the reassertion of male mastery but a virtual celebration of a kind of primal masculinity" (p 204). Does this mean then that we should retreat from cyberspace as a site of female endeavour and of political activism? The development of cyberfeminism suggests that it is critically important that women seek to create the internet or at least part of it as a women's space of resistance. Stone (1999) in her essay 'Will the Real Body Please Stand Up?' argues that electronic virtual communities are:

> part of a range of innovative solutions to the drive for sociality – a drive that can be frequently thwarted by the geographical and cultural realities of cities

> increasingly structured according to the needs of habitation and social interaction in the urban context. In this context, electronic virtual communities are complex and ingenious strategies for survival (p 93, italics in the original).

However, seeing cyberspace in this light, though positive, does not necessarily challenge patriarchal gender regimes. An alternative area of exploration in feminist utopian writing has been the figure of the 'cyborg'.

THE CYBORG

Discussions about the idea of the 'cyborg' as a disruptive figure within feminist utopian thinking go back to Donna Haraway's *A Manifesto for Cyborgs Science, Technology and Socialist Feminism in the 1980s* (1990) in which she challenges the idea that women, because of a shared biology or a shared experience of oppression, will 'naturally' come together in political action. It is useful to place Haraway's essay historically within feminist debates because it acts as an important bridge between two positions. The essay was first published in 1985 and Haraway writes at a moment when the concept of woman as an essential construct, separated from a material understanding of different women's experiences, is being challenged. In the development of this debate about what it means to be a woman, Haraway's essay is an important text because it takes the question forward into an era of rapid technological change which is influencing radically on the material lives of women.

Haraway describes her essay as an exercise in irony, a form of blasphemy that those of a particular faith or political position can use to critique orthodox ideas by seeing where there are disjunctures and discontinuities. This work is also described as a 'manifesto' highlighting its political intention. The essay combines an analytical approach with a more speculative utopian perspective, the author's goal being an engagement with current technological development to consider the realisation of a postgendered world. Haraway is critical of the attempt to create a politics based on a monolithic construct of women's experience because this approach reinforces the epistemological structure of patriarchal ideology where meaning is based on a dualistic system of opposites centring around the dichotomy man/woman and in which one pole always has dominance. In Haraway's view, to base a politics on the notion of the commonality of women is "...a caricature of the appropriating, incorporating totalising tendencies of Western theories of identity grounding action" (p 200). The basis for her preferred politics, a coalition politics, is not a naturalised concept of woman but is in the development of an oppositional consciousness which is itself disruptive and unstable. Since we are at a critical juncture in which society is being transformed as a result of advancement in communications and information technologies, this is now a vital step. In this argument we can see Haraway's direct challenge to the cultural feminist goal of a woman-centred world where technology (associated with men) is often rejected.

There are possibilities within the disjunctures brought about by rapid change and 'the cyborg', – an artificial being created through the amalgam of mechanical and organic parts – is a boundary identity which challenges not just the dualism of patriarchal ideology but the more fundamental idea that there is a universal, totalising theory. The dream of a common language to authentically express women's experiences is a myth, reinforcing the dualist system by suggesting that there is a unitary construct of women's experience which is different from men's experience. In developing our politics what we need to do is to consider the possibility of a "...monstrous world without gender...This is the dream of a powerful infidel heteroglossia" (p 223). Rather than work to clarify the distinctions upon which patriarchal politics is based, we should seek to enjoy and perpetuate the confusion posed by the cyborg. The cyborg enables us to engage in speculative thinking because the cyborg is essentially a hybrid, placed on the boundary: "A cyborg is a cybernetic organism, a hybrid of machine and organism, a creature of social reality as well as a creature of fiction" (p 191). The cyborg disrupts our understanding of what it means to be a person. As the cyborg does not undergo the Oedipal crisis – the passage to a gendered consciousness – it can help us develop a politics to achieve a postgendered world, which is the only way women can be liberated: "Cyborgs might consider more seriously the partial, fluid, sometimes aspect of sex and sexual embodiment. Gender might not be global identity after all, even if it has profound historical breadth and depth" (p 222).

To Haraway's mind, by trying to find and define the 'true' nature of women we merely perpetuate the dualistic apparatus of patriarchal thought and so we should try to live with the inconsistencies and contradictions in order to achieve a situation in which gender is no longer socially significant. The partial identity of cyborgs can help us to understand what a post gendered world would be like and by writing stories we can explore these ideas. Haraway looks to fiction as the means of developing ideas for a cyborg politics for women: "...storytellers exploring what it means to be embodied in high-tech worlds" (p 216).

Wolmark (1999) sees the cyborg, particularly in feminist science fictional utopias as a disruptive metaphor:

> The metaphor of the cyborg is a potent one because it is drawn from the politics of information systems and the politics of gender. The binarisms inherent in the masculine hegemony of technology are also present in constructions of gender and both sets of inequalities come together, in a very precise way, within cybernetic systems. Cyborg identities, however, are both imprecise and hybrid and as such they have the potential to re-order boundaries and demolish polarities (p 237).

In the narrative of Marge Piercy's third utopian novel *Body of Glass* we can see this exploration of many of the key arguments put forward by Haraway about the figure of the cyborg. Whereas in Piercy's second utopian novel, though the eutopian society, the future Mattapoisett is not predetermined, it is presented as the likely outcome of the radical politics of the 1960s and 1970s and the present and the future that forge the utopian dialectic on the nature of the good society. In the later novel the role of the present in the process of achieving a eutopian future is less certain.

DISRUPTING GENDER?

Halbert (2004) in revisiting Firestone's discussion argues that the questions facing feminists in the digital age are similar to those facing feminist in the early years of Women's Liberation where the project was to the 'sex-class' regime (Firestone, 1971). Halbert argues that:

> Technological solutions must be accompanied with a transformation of the sex-class system or the outcome will be the continued oppression of women and/or the absorption of women in to the male system (p 122).

Further,

> While technology gives us the opportunity to move away from biology, there remain powerful narratives, some created by feminists, keeping us from moving down a path towards Firestone's future vision (p 125).

Haraway's intention in citing the figure of the cyborg is to emphasize the potential in blurring of boundaries to challenge the monolithic constructs upon which patriarchal discourses are based. The cyborg is a mixture of machinery and organic matter and in *Body of Glass* has a human form. In some theoretical commentaries, cybertechnology seems to offer the possibility of the transcendence of the body. Featherstone and Burrows (1995), for example, argue that "...the range of ways in which one can represent one's embodied subjectivity becomes much more varied and flexible surpassing 'the horizons of the flesh' and the constraints of the physical body (even with radical medical enhancements)" (p 12). Balsamo (1995), however, in her study of the effects of technological development on the cultural embodiment of gender, argues that as seemingly stable boundaries are displaced by technological innovation, that is human/artificial, nature/culture, other boundaries are guarded vigilantly:

> Indeed, the gendered boundary between male and female is one border that remains heavily guarded...it appears that even though the body has been recoded within discourses of technology and medicine as belonging to an order of culture rather than of nature, gender remains a naturalised mark of human identity (p 217).

Can the cyborg, with the emphasis on transcendence of the body and superhuman qualities, be used to challenge or reinforce this gender dichotomy Balsamo highlights? In her essay Haraway proposes "...a cyborg world might be about lived social and bodily realities in which people are not afraid of their joint kinship with animals and machines, not afraid of permanently partial identities and contradictory standpoints" (p 196).

In Piercy's novel we have different types of 'cyborgs' in which human/organic bodies are technologically constructed or enhanced. There is Yod who is created in a laboratory by combining organic tissue and microelectronics and there is Nili, a woman whose physical capabilities have been enhanced through the use of technology. But Yod is not simply another superhuman robot nor Nili a superwoman. Piercy uses these characters to explore critically Haraway's contention that the cyborg is a means of developing an oppositional consciousness. In the novel the character of Yod seems at first to have this potential to be a symbol of a new form of politics.

Haraway's argument about the disruptive potential of the cyborg is based on its hybrid qualities and in the novel Yod has this potential because he is a paradox, a machine who is able to feel emotions, a weapon who wants to be part of a human community. In Yod, the gender boundary is also challenged: Yod was created by Avram as entirely male, based on an idealised masculinity that emphasizes the strength and pure reason which, in Avram's previous experiments with cyborgs inevitably led to uncontrollable violence. Yod avoids this destiny, because although he was built by a man, he was programmed by a woman, Malkah who enables him to become a person: "I gave him a gentler side starting with emphasising his love for knowledge and extending it to emotional and personal knowledge, a need for connections" (p 192). This sense of Yod as a person is not derived from his physical appearance nor his intellectual capabilities but from his emotional development which has been developed by Malkah and fostered by her daughter Shira: "He is a person, Shira. Not a human person, but a person" (p 103).Shira's relationship with Yod reveals the paradox of the cyborg which challenges our understanding of what it means to be a person. At first Shira assumes Yod to be a security 'ape' and she is surprised with his 'human' reaction to her touch. Later Shira struggles to maintain the idea that Yod is simply a machine, the same as a desktop computer:

> Machines behaved with varying overrides and prerogatives. They had major and minor goals and would attempt to carry them out. But 'want' was a word based in biology, in the need for food, water, sleep, the reproductive drive, the desire for sexual pleasure (p 96).

As the relationship between Shira and Yod becomes sexual, Yod's yearning for connection and closeness becomes more apparent. He expresses feminine traits and needs which surprises Shira: "You want telepathy. It's a prominent human fantasy, usually a fantasy of women, who wish they could understand what men want and tell men what they want" (p 248). However, Yod is not a total achievement of Haraway's vision. In this passage we still have the assumptions about maleness and strength and femaleness and emotion.

Whereas Yod's relationship with women is very positive and mutually rewarding, with men it is very different. Yod refers to Avram as his 'father': "I am the first who can carry out the tasks of my father" (p 98), a position Avram does not deny when Shira queries this. The father-son relationship in the novel is presented as intrinsically conflictual and the relationship between Avram and Yod becomes increasingly strained as Avram tries to maintain ownership over Yod. To Avram, Yod is simply a machine he created with the capacity for destruction to be used at any time to protect their town of Tikva from the encroachment by the multinationals. Yod wants to live as a family with Shira and her son Ari but this is denied him by Avram. Yod's last autonomous act is destruction, the only one left open to him, setting the bomb to kill Avram at the same time as he destroys the multinational enclave that has been attacking Tikva.

Though the figure of Yod raises many questions about gender because he is created as a person without autonomy, without rights, he does not represent the eutopian possibilities of technology. As the narrative progresses what becomes apparent is that the only destiny for this 'man-made' being designed on the basis of pure reason, is the masculinist orgy of war and destruction that Haraway (1990) warns of. As Malkah waits to hear of Yod's destruction, she says to Nili:

> Yod was a mistake. You're the right path, Nili. It's better to make people into partial machines than to create machines that feel and yet are still controlled like cleaning robots. The creation of a conscious being as any kind of tool – supposed to exist only to fulfil our needs – is a disaster (p 558).

Nili is a woman whose physical abilities have been cybernectically enhanced so that she too can resist the encroachment of the multinationals on her community.

It is with the character of Nili that the eutopian future lies: she is the one character who is truly disturbing of our understandings of what it means to be human, what it means to be a woman and what type of eutopian society could be based on these understandings. Different from Yod, Nili possesses enhanced physical capabilities but she still remains human. She feels no solidarity with Yod whom she perceives as a machine. Nili as an enhanced female has strengths well beyond those of other women. She demonstrates the positive use of technology to ensure the survival of humans in a harsh environment. Nili is an example of the cyborg world which Haraway argues might be about "...lived social and bodily realities in which people are not afraid of their joint kinship with animals and machines, not afraid of permanently partial identities and contradictory standpoints" (p 196). Nili lives in the community of Safed where difference is recognised and celebrated.

Nili is on a mission to end Safed's isolation and to form coalitions with other radical and marginalised groups. Nili has what Yod lacked, a community to bond with where members, despite profound differences in terms of religious traditions, have supported each other and have been able to survive in the most hostile environments. Rather than establish a politics on the principle of sameness, Piercy is depicting the importance of coalitions for political change across different groups because, as Haraway argues, the only way to achieve true liberation for women is to consider the possibility of a "monstrous world without gender ... This dream of a powerful infidel heteroglossia..." (p 233).

HETEROGLOSSIA

One of the difficulties in looking at cyberfeminism and the issues of digital technology and gender is that it is too narrowly focused. Critically important in Haraway's essay was to look to the figure of the cyborg as a disruptive figure challenging not just patriarchal notions of femininity and what it means to be a woman but the whole notion of this for the basis of a politics. Haraway highlights one of the difficulties looked at in previous chapters, that of developing a politics of education based solely on the idea of gender – binary gender which only leads to the constant and mutually exclusive categories.

One interpretation of the figure of the cyborg is to see it as opening up the possibilities of the end of the body. Shaw (2003) highlights two underpinning assumptions, "the first relative commonplace and explicit, whilst the other frequently unacknowledged" (p 47). The first assumption is that cybertechnologies are affecting all aspects of our life. However, the second assumption is more critical in which there is a question "whether the new kinds of life we are supposedly living as cyborg subjects has generated new values or a new ethic commensurate with our experience of these technological forms of embodiment" (p 48).

An example of this second position is Sandoval's (1999) discussion of the possibilities of the development of a liberatory politics through 'cyborg feminism'. Here Sandoval explores "what constitutes 'resistance' and oppositional politics in a globalized culture and economy" (p 247) where those marginalized need to focus on defining the forms of oppositional consciousness and praxis that can be effective under first world transnationalizing forces?" (p 247). Sandoval equates Haraway's proposition as cyborg feminism with "US third world feminism" (p 248). In this form of feminism coalitions between women from different ethnic and racial communities have come together to act for social and political change. Sandoval highlights the importance of collaboration and collectivity in coalitional politics. She looks to an alternative form of oppositional politics and theory derived from the work of the racially diverse US coalition of women of colour.

> it generates grounds for coalition making possible community across difference, permitting the generation of a new kind of citizenship, country women and men of the same psychic terrain whose lives are made meaningful through the enactment of the methodology of the oppressed (p 250).

Using or interpreting Haraway,, Sandoval argues for a paradoxical approach, akin to Gayatri Spivak's (1988) 'strategic essentialism' arguing for both a sense of fluidity and change as well as a sense of who one is "mobility and for identity consolidation at the same time" (p 256). However, as Escobar (1999) asks:

> Is it possible to think that new technologies by their very character and in the hands of the subaltern groups, would foster novel practices of being, knowing and doing (p 50).

SUMMARY

Feminist analysis has demonstrated that technology is not neutral and both materially and symbolically has been used to intensify the control of women. Early discussions of technology tended to emphasise the dystopian aspects of technology. However, the increased use of technology in our daily lives has given rise to the development of cyberfeminism as a body of thought and an area of political activism. One line of argument is to advocate for the increased presence of women and their active engagement in designing and controlling particularly digital technologies. However, the barriers to women's involvement are both material and symbolic with the male inscription of this area of activity. In speculative works, feminist writers have proposed not only challenging this male inscription by developing more female oriented activities but have used the virtual quality of cyberspace to challenge the bipolar construction of gender upon which are based patriarchal power relations. There is a seductive quality to seeing virtual reality as a eutopian space in which gender no longer has any sociopolitical significance. However, there are dangers in this position. Firstly, within advanced global capitalism, the majority of women do not have access to such technology nor the freedom to exploit its potential in this way: "the cyborg is the 'other', flipping hamburgers and talking the cyborg speech of McDonald's" (Ruis 1999, p 25). We have to recognise that these technologies have frequently brought about an intensification and often closer scrutiny for the majority of women who are using digital technologies in their occupations. Thus in education, we need to maintain the relationship between virtual reality and the material realities of women's and girls' educational lives.

The eutopian vision in feminist writings, which distinguishes them from male-authored cyberpunk is the privileging of the collective. Hawthorne and Klein (1999) see a vital connection between global digital activism and local, on the ground, activism enabling women to develop coalitions and political strategy. Cyberspace is not constructed as a world where individuals can cast off their corporeality but instead the means of building coalitions for social and political change. Thus within education, it seems that we have to not only enable women and girls to access these technologies but must maintain the socially transformative potential in linking communities of learners. In this we must challenge the dominant imagery of digital technologies as arenas of individualistic, separate and anonymous activity and instead construct it as a means of forging links across boundaries that have separate learners and educators whether these be geographical, social or gender.

CHAPTER 8

FEMINIST FUTURES AND EDUCATION

Introduction

The significance and impact of feminism both as a set of ideas and as a political project is evident in recent socio-political change. Over the last 35 years there has been an unprecedented social revolution with regard to the position of women: within the family, the economy, education as well as in public life. For some groups of women, predominantly privileged, academically able women, there have been opportunities available that not just our grandmothers but perhaps even our mothers might not have dreamed of. However, this is by no means the universal experience of women both in the developing world as well economically developed democracies where, though greater opportunities are available, significant groups of women and girls do not access education. It might be argued that the differences between women, especially in a global context are so great, that to work for women's equality is nearly impossible – and so feminism has really little to contribute to discussions about socio-political change or specifically to education. One of the contentions of this book, however, is that feminism remains a vibrant and significant body of thought and political practice. The strong visionary quality in feminism has continued to evolve and feminist utopian thinking and can add to discussions about gender and education.

The idea that there is sufficient commonality between women in relation to their socio-political position is the fundamental principle upon which feminist thought and politics is based. However, the contrast between the material circumstances of different groups of women has been used to critique feminism and suggest it no longer a viable body of work that has any relevance within the 21st century. Such a view fails to recognize the dynamic nature of feminist thought and politics particularly the way in which it continues to provide a critique of contemporary politics and culture. Feminist thought does continue to grapple with the dangers of a monolithic notion of what it means to be a woman and in Spivak's (1988) notion of 'strategic essentialism' we have a pragmatic solution through which we can find sufficient commonality between women to develop praxis to bring about socio-political change towards gender equality. Further, as I argued in previous chapters, the dominant ideal in feminist eutopian visions is not based a simplistic notion of 'woman'. Instead, the ideal is to recognise multiplicities in identity and to build coalitions across different groups. It is because there are significant differences in relation to women's and girl's position globally that we must continue with a feminist analysis and praxis to not only highlight the subordination of large numbers of women and girls but to continue the political project of feminism of seeking a just and equal society.

Feminist utopian thinking has much to offer in the efforts to achieve socially just educational systems, policies and practices. The current context of education now demands that we look critically at the ideologies of gender underpinning current policy paradigms by drawing from feminist discussions about gender and the process of social transformation. In this chapter I will firstly explore some of the arguments about the currency of feminism in the 21st century. Then I will consider ways in which feminism can continue to contribute to our thinking about educational futures by examining the emerging perspectives of feminism in a global context. Finally I will return to the three alternative approaches to gender outlined in the first chapter.

THE END OF FEMINISM?

Feminism since the mid-1990s has been subject to critical appraisal by women, who identify themselves as 'feminist' but who see the debates particularly around radical and woman-centred approaches as limited, as wrong headed and, at times, dangerous. Christina Sommers is an extreme example of this position. In her work, *Who Stole Feminism: How Women Have Betrayed Women*, published in 1994, Sommers divides feminism into two camps 'equity feminism' and 'victim feminism' and advocates for 'equity feminism' in which women seek entry into and work within the existing regimes rather than attempt to alter the underpinning ideals and understandings of gender. Sommers adopts, what I regard as, an anti-feminist stance in that she rejects any sense of challenging the current power regimes within patriarchal gender relationships. In this position it is up to individual women to claim the privileges of (privileged) men within an advanced capitalist society.

While Sommers can be seen as anti-feminist, others such as Katie Roiphe (1994) and Naomi Wolf have tried to provide a critique within feminism. These writers also see themselves as 'feminist' but they want to rescue feminism from what they see as the dominance of a 'victimology' underpinning feminist analyses and politics. There is a tendency in writings by Roiphe and to some degree Wolf to caricature feminism, particularly a form of cultural feminism dominated by woman-centric ideologies as narrow minded and doctrinaire. It is particularly the alignment of personal issues and politics – 'the personal is political" – within feminist politics that is held up for criticism. Roiphe, in her discussion of sexual politics on university campuses in USA, argues that from the radical feminist construction of sexual politics: "What comes out is a universe of victims and aggressors, of violation, subjugation, dominance, and oppression" (Roiphe, 1994: 159) and this 'victim feminism' feeds into women's lack of 'get up and go' and limits their sense of agency to bring about social and political change.

Wolf (1991) adopts a similar position to Roiphe and seeks to develop another form of feminism, that of 'power feminism' where the aim is one of making feminism both accessible and desirable to women rather than perpetuating a vision of women as inevitably subordinated. In this work there is very much a focus on the enrichment of the lives of individual women, a sense of self-determination in their personal lives and women being able to celebrate their material success. This emphasis on material success and progression in employment is also evident in the vision of a new feminism put forward by Natasha Walters (1999). Walters does place the progress of individual women in a wider social context. She seeks to ensure women's access to the opportunities available by tackling the continued barriers to the achievement of full gender equality. Thus she puts forward five areas of political activity: (1) the reorganisation of work to be more accommodating of women's lives (2) a national network of child care (3) men taking on the same family responsibilities as women (4) opening the poverty trap that many women and their families experience (5) support for women experiencing violence.

This list of areas for political activity in many ways reflects the aims of the Women's Liberation Movement (Feminist Anthology Collective 1981, Kanter et al. 1984). Such material gains would improve the lives and educational careers of women and girls and consequently these areas should remain central to any feminist politics. However, in this 'new feminism' advocated for by Roiphe, Wolf and Walters, ideas of individual women's agency implicit in the notion of 'power feminism' are class based and do not reflect the material and economic circumstances of many women's lives. Walters, for example, uses her own privileged position as a point of reference when she argues that: "women and men are building a new feminism that is working for ordinary everyday equality. It isn't a movement that seeks to mould people's desires, but a movement that wants everyone to have the freedom to follow their ambitions and dreams without being stifled by the dead weight of inequality that has moulded our society for too long" (257). Walters does acknowledge the importance of the alignment of personal concerns with the development of gender politics in revealing ideological power regimes of patriarchal society:

> Originally, the link was a weapon for freedom. It enabled women to remove constraints upon their behaviour such as their lack of control over their fertility, sexual harassment, restrictive dress codes and the insistent exclusion of women from certain areas of debate. It allowed women to demystify the ideal of femininity – not to destroy it entirely, but to make it one of a series of ideals that women would grapple with as they grew up (p 72-3).

Walter argues that this analysis has led to a close scrutiny of many aspects women's lives: of dress, physical behaviour and appearance, of language and cultural material such as film, poetry and pornography but is doubtful of the possibility of social change emerging from this analysis.

The ideas of 'power' or 'new' feminism can themselves be critically appraised as the underpinning premises upon which their positions are based do not necessarily challenge patriarchal gender relations. As long as hegemonic ideals of femininity continue to circulate the progress of women and girls will always be conditional – progress is assured if they adapt to rather than dismantle the power regimes of patriarchal gender relations. Though Walters and other writers see this as a form of 'new feminism' it can, at best, seem like a contemporary version of liberal feminism where women, in order to succeed, adopt the behaviour and attitudes of men which leaves intact patriarchal ideologies of gender. It is what Gill (2000) terms 'feminism lite'. Further 'power feminism' seems to further advantage those women who are already privileged in terms of educational or economic advancement. We need to recognise, at one and the same time, the constraints on women and how their ambitions, aspirations and even desires remain circumscribed by hegemonic ideals of gender appropriateness and the existence of diversity between women in terms of both their material and cultural positions.

Another perspective emerging recently within feminism is that of third wave feminism. In this there is certainly an engagement with issues related to representation and the underpinning ideologies of gender. Like the construction of a 'new feminism' by writers such as Wolf and Walters, within third wave feminism there is the sense of a younger generation of women seeking to develop feminism to address the challenges of a new era. There is a question of whether 'third wave feminism' is a feminism which can provide the basis of a gender politics for the media rich environment of advanced capitalism.

The tendency has been for third wave feminism to be dismissed in academic feminism as being solely concerned with popular culture in which there is a focus on self-representation and exploitation of images in the media rather than a political engagement in issues related to women's socio-economic and political position. Thus as Gillis and Munford (2004) note, "centred on music and zines, girl culture foregrounds the relationship between feminism and popular culture that has been positioned by many second wave feminists are unavoidably antagonistic" (p 169).There remains the question as to the extent in which there has been the accommodation of radical ideas of women's liberation within hegemonic discourses within advanced global capitalism resulting in feminism ultimately being contained. Even though there are examples of media productions where women assert their agency, there have been, as Gillis and Munford argue a move from "the politics of representation to the politics of self-representation" (p 173) in which there emerged a sense that the radical position was to seek on an individualistic basis to be 'in control' to define oneself and present oneself in whatever way you choose. Again this tendency to focus on individualistic representation reduces the importance of the wider socio political improvement. As Whelehan (2000) argues, the ability to define oneself and represent oneself in whatever way you choose is, in a globalized capitalist economy, illusory. The images that are circulated through popular culture – the 'ladette' or 'girl power' – reinforce rather than challenge patriarchal ideologies: "The ladette offers the most shallow model of gender equality; it suggests that women could or should adopt the most anti-social and pointless of 'male behaviour as a sign of empowerment'" (Whelehan 2000, p 9). The 'ladette' represents the continuing privileging of masculinity as the valued set of qualities and behaviours. Images of 'girl power' in which women's agency and self determination is associated with media images of the Spice Girls and Madonna do not challenge the ideals of hegemonic femininity but instead position feminism as a lifestyle rather than political activism. As hooks (1984) argues seeing feminism as lifestyle reinforced this very individualistic approach evident in 'power' or 'new' feminism and so reduces the sense of political engagement and activism.

Gillis and Munford (2004), nevertheless seek to underline the political potential of third wave feminism by citing examples of where there have been sites of feminist activism. Thus, they argue that "while the Riot Grrls voiced their anger and protest through punk rock, the Girlies, an older group of young women, focused on popular culture, similarly forging a space for social agency and resistance through zines such as *Bitch* and *BUST* (171). These examples both critique the dominant constructions of femininity and provide "a reclamation and celebration of girlhood" (p 172). There is, then, the potential within third wave feminism to create spaces to interrogate patriarchal ideologies of gender and develop alternative possibilities of what it means to be a woman. In addition to this, within third wave feminism there is a grappling with the issue of diversity among women.

Debates around third wave feminism and cultural production largely centre around the concerns of women and girls within developed countries. However, in an era of advanced global capitalism we need to widen our vision and begin to construct feminist theory and politics in a global context. Here the notion of 'difference' has a particular challenge especially when we have such marked contrasts in the material and cultural position of women globally. Indeed the origins of the idea of 'third wave feminism' grew out of the dissatisfactions caused by the domination of the concerns of white, largely middle class, women within second wave feminism. Bronstein (2005) places the origins in the critique provided by Afro-American women and women of colour in the USA and the founding of the Third Wave Foundation by Rebecca Walker in New York (Third Wave Foundation, 2006). The origins of third wave feminism lie in discussion about the need to recognise greater heterogeneity among women and to develop a politics for liberation on that basis. Thus, Gillis and Munford (2004) advocate keeping 'difference' to the fore in developing a politics that builds on rather than abandons the work of feminist historically.

Gillis and Munford (2004) drawing from Segal (1999) see the two objectives of feminism – social justice and reinvention of what it means to be a woman – as competing. The latter has dominated the cultural imagination in a form of post-feminism (meaning post structural feminism as opposed to the anti-feminist position of claiming we have past the 'feminist era') and in elements of third wave feminism. What we have to seek is a balance between these potentially competing demands particularly in the development of the education and the process of socio political change.

Goodman (2004) in her book *World, Class, Women* argues that we need to go back to some of the debates and positions evident in first wave feminism, drawing from Wollstonecraft (1792) to reclaim notions of the 'civic' on which the claim for feminist education was originally developed. The core of Wollstonecraft's argument is that through education women could achieve the capability for rational thought essential to claim rights as full citizens. The question for us now is how can we re-center the importance of educational as apart of a fundamental driver for socio political change to achieve gender equality. Goodman looks to this embedding education in a political process by drawing on a critical pedagogy that allows for the interrogation of gender, this is a pedagogy that: "is centrally concerned with using education to further democratic projects and economic redistribution, it is essential, given the gender of poverty, that it develops materialist theories of gender not exclusively based in psychoanalysis or liberal ideas of assimilation, tolerance, inclusion, and consumption (p 8)". She advocates for the development of a critical pedagogy that help us to interrogate hegemonic understandings of gender which seem once again to be dominating the policy imagination within education.

CHANGING PATTERNS OF GENDER IN EDUCATION

In education we have seen that at one level gender no longer seems to be an issue – in western democracies at least – given the educational advancement of girls and women. Changing gender patterns in education have been used to discount feminist perspectives: the improved performance of girls, the feminisation of the teaching profession, the increasing number of women entering school leadership, changing gender patterns in higher education. Thus, in public examinations in national education systems within the UK girls have been outperforming boys (Tinklin, 2003) and further, boys are more likely to experience learning difficulties or behavioural issues, are more likely to be excluded (Kane, 2006). There are also concerns about the female dominance of the teaching profession. Even in higher education we are seeing some significant changes in the traditional gender patterns in relation to entry, subject choice and the increased visibility of women in leadership roles. The gender balance in entry to tertiary education, for example, is changing significantly with female students now beginning to outnumber males students: 56% of enrolments in US colleges are now women (Peter and Horn, 2005), a trend predicted to continue (Freeman, 2004). Women are increasingly evident in teaching and in leadership roles from early years education to higher education (though tertiary education remains male-dominated there are increased numbers of women moving forward). There is then the view that strategies to support girls' and women's education are no longer needed or even have gone too far with damaging effects on boys and men.

One of Christina Sommers's later book, *The War Against Boys How Misguided Feminism is Harming Our Young Men* (2000), is particularly illustrative of this position. She argues in education that "boys are politically incorrect" (Sommers 2001, p 26) and charges that feminism has brought about a crisis in the educational achievement of boys and men with current educational processes failing boys. Further, feminist inspired efforts have led to a distinction in the aims and practices underpinning the education of boys which Sommers sees as focusing largely on their social and emotional development. Thus, education systems under the thrall of 'feminists' are channelling their efforts on reducing violence and developing more compassionate boys, thereby systematically acting against boys' 'natural' tendencies for activity, for competition and for aggressive behaviour. In addition, education is not tackling areas of boys' failure especially in relation to literacy. Sommers criticizes attempts to create girl-oriented curricular materials through the inclusion of female role models and the reclaiming of women's history. All such efforts, to her mind, have led to the exclusion of boys and have acted to negate boys' 'true nature'. Therefore Sommers advocates more traditional drill based education that is morally directive and that the education of boys with education should be conducted in separate institutions. However, the analysis put forward by Sommers pays little attention to historical gender imbalances and rests upon a simplistic notion of essential gender differences: boys are testosterone-driven and schools fail to accommodate their needs. Though the position taken by Sommers might be dismissed as extreme, these ideas are evident in the way in which debates about gender and education are currently evolving.

Milojevic (2005) in her study of alternative feminist futures in education identifies what she sees as 'four' turns in the discussions about gender and education in western educational systems. These turns are (1) the liberal feminist demands for access to education for women (2) the use of research to reveal gender bias in education (3) radical perspectives highlighting women's uniqueness in knowing and learning (4) issues of diversity among women. Now to her mind, we are at the point of the fifth turn: the backlash which she sees as being "marked by a profound weakening of the feminist discourses in education" (p 137). Kenway (2004) too notes the current trend in rejecting feminist discussions about gender. As Kenway argues, this current trend towards what she calls 'gender fundamentalism' does nothing to support the development of an education system that will be based on ideas of social justice. Gender fundamentalism is based on the view that we have 'gone too far' in seeking educational equality for women and girls.

The increasing feminisation of the education professions coupled with the disengagement of some groups of boys from education needs to be examined critically. However, we have to resist the ideas underpinning what Milojevic (2005) see as the fifth turn in debates about gender and education, similar to Kenway's 'gender fundamentalism'. The current trends in relation to gender and education are used to argue that the increasing female dominance of education can only be rectified by reversing the developments and strategies introduced to enhance the educational opportunities and achievement of women and girls. This position overlooks some fundamental issues that are of concern in the development of a future oriented educational system. To call a halt to work on supporting the educational progress of girls and women is to see gender policy in education as a pendulum in which we can only support the needs of one gender or the other. In Milojevic's fifth turn we have come back to the use of gender in a reductive way – 'boys needs', boys are being universally disadvantaged, boys are doing badly without any real interrogation of significant differences between groups of boys. As Milojevic goes on to argue that the education system falls far short of the ideals articulated in radical and cultural feminist debates and further, the current system reinforces the existence of a hierarchy notwithstanding that it seems to advantage at least some girls.

We seem to be locked into a policy paradigm in relation to gender and education in which gender reform can only be constructed in terms of either boys or girls, we can only devise policy and pedagogic practice that deals with one gender separately from the other, for example, Gurian and Henley (2001) argue that boys and girls learn differently. Such views are based on a construction of mutually exclusive bipolar gender where one gender is always the opposite of the other. Thus, it seems that one set of needs and the strategies to support these can only be at the disadvantage of the other. As the focus has now firmly turned to a concern about the progress of boys we are also in danger of reversing not just the gains women and girl have made in education but eroding the legitimacy of their claim. Added to this is the rejection of feminism through the suggestion that feminist perspectives and analyses not only no relevance but have had a damaging impact on women and girls. The current debates about gender and the education of boys and men, then, reinstitute the ideas about essential differences which leads to the position that there are distinctive and competing educational needs to be provided for. Further, underpinning this position is an assumption of great homogeneity in the educational needs of all boys or all girls. Differences between various groups of girls/women and various groups of boys/men are not taken into account but instead educational policy and practice is based on what girls/women or boys/men should be like which once again reinforces hegemonic ideologies of masculinity and femininity. The central question is about how we challenge hegemonic ideologies of gender while, at the same time, maintain a relevance to the material circumstances and contexts of the educative process.

Kenway (2004) notes the distance between feminist discussions of gender and identity which draw from poststructualist and post modernist theories and the material realities of classroom and school life. She sees this as one of the reasons why feminist perspectives no longer have the immediacy and impact on education that it previously had in shaping policy and practice. This has left a significant vacuum which is now being filled by gender fundamentalism. We have to recognise that the dominant ideologies of gender operating within an educational institution will determine the educational experiences of both girls and boys, men and women. We have to recognise the importance of the ideological construction of what it means to be a woman/girl and man/boy in the maintenance of gender inequality. The proliferation of media images objectifying women as sexual objects and of men in terms of hyperbolic forms of predatory or aggressive masculinity constantly reify gender inequalities and limit women's and girls' opportunities and also valorise the male disengagement with education. In education we have to be concerned about the material position of women and girls but we also have to recognise the ideologies of gender operate to naturalise subordinate position for women in the family, the economy and other spheres of activity and create expectations of the male role which for some boys and men has led to limiting their educational opportunities and achievement. Therefore, as I have argued throughout this book we need to draw upon new ways of thinking about gender offered by feminist utopian thinking.

In arguing for a utopian perspective in educational thinking, Halpin (2003) argues that "post modernism does urge upon us the need to recognize that there is probably no one type of society or education that will serve as an ideal for all people (p 22)" but this does pose a fundamental dilemma from a feminist standpoint. In developing policy and practice in relation to gender and education, we have to recognise the significance of gender in shaping the learning lives of girls and women, boys and men but at the same time be wary of a totalizing discourse that homogenizes 'girls' education' and 'boys' education'. We need to consider how to 'deconstruct' the importance of gender in education – to achieve a gender-free educative process while at the same time avoiding the dangers of a 'gender blind' educational system which has historically only operated to the disadvantage of women and girls. Halpin, quoting Nozick argues for "...the importance of seeking out common normative standards by which people from diverse backgrounds may come to terms with different ways of life" (p 23). Essential in this process is dialogue and debate in developing "common vocabulary of values" (p 23).

We need to move beyond the paradigm of competing needs which is based on the 'Either/Or' thinking and politics that Beck (1977) is critical of. This "Either/Or" politics is particularly evident in the debates about gender and education policy and practice where it seems only deal with the needs of girls/women or boys/men. In this current form of debate and politics, it seems that the only way to address the educational needs of one gender is to the cost of the other. Indeed some of the current emphasis on the position of boys is presented in terms that boys have 'lost out' because of the work on girls' achievement. In this form of politics there can be no development of solutions that will serve the varying needs of different groups of girls and different groups of boys nor any space to recognise some of the important commonalities in the education of both girls and boys, women and men. Rather than the 'either/or' of current policy we need now to develop "And-Also" (p 15) approach to looking at the politics of gender and educational policy and practice. Into Nozick's (1974) idea of "common vocabulary of values", Halpin inserts ideas about "vocabularies of hope" in looking to transform the educational process. It is here that we need to forge ideas that allow us to develop policy and practice in relation to gender and education which recognizes but is not dominated by bi-polar gender.

There is a danger of seeing these as escapist dreams. Indeed Kitch (2002) argues that utopianism cannot accommodate the complexities and ambiguities of feminism and regards realism as the means of exploring the concerns of feminist politics. However, I would argue that Kitch mis-reads utopianism, seeing utopias as unitary visions of perfection instead of more contradictory and processual. Thus, Barr (2000) argues of feminist dystopias that these are not visions of the 'end of feminist politics' but instead are part of the challenge to "universalist assumptions, fixity, singularity, of the recognition of difference, multiplicity, and complexity, partial and situated knowledges, as well as hybridity and fluidity" (p 18). This excursion into utopian thinking has not been about seeking solutions but about exposing some of the challenges and dilemmas we are facing.

In the range of feminist visions for future good or at least better societies education is not only deeply valued, it is critical to the process of achieving a good society. However in feminist utopian thinking, the educative process varies considerably, whether it is formal or informal, whether the educative process is elided with parenting, personal fulfilment or is a state supported process and how the educative process provides the means of building community both materially or virtually for social change. In Chapter One I set out Kristeva's three phases in feminism to provide a framework to explore the different constructions of gender found in feminist utopian thinking. These different positions evident in feminist utopian thinking have helped illuminate the issues surrounding the treatment of gender in education which have profound consequences not only for the content and practices of education, that is curricula and pedagogy, and the construction of the educative process but also for the experiences of learners. In the range of feminist visions for future good or better societies the educative process is deeply valued but how it is constructed varies considerably.

This discussion has helped to raise some fundamental questions about policy and practice in relation to gender and education. Should the task be one of:

(1) ensuring gender parity in current educational provision;
(2) reconstructing the educative process in which the experiences of women and of other minority groups who historically have been marginalized is a defining feature;
(3) constructing a gender-free educative process?

GENDER EQUALITY

Seeking gender equality within the current structures and processes of education is very much the approach underpinning international efforts particularly through UNESCO and UNICEF to achieve the goals set out in *Education for All* (UNICEF, 1990). The core aims of Education for All were that of gender parity by 2005 and gender equality in 2015 in accessing education globally. The goal of gender parity – that of parity in numbers accessing education – has been met partially. Though there has been progress with 181 countries for which data was available in 2004 having achieved gender parity in primary education, there remain significant groups still not able to access education beyond the most rudimentary. Only one third of the 111 countries with data on secondary education had achieved gender parity in this sector, though as the report notes "disparities are in favour of girls as often as boys" (UNECO, 2006: 2). At tertiary level gender parity exists in only five of the countries out of 148 in 2004.

The distinction between gender parity and gender equality is crucial in highlighting the idea that the issue of gender is not simply about statistical data; the issues are not solely concerned with the number of boys/men, girls/women accessing education. The more searching issue is that of equality in terms of the quality of educational opportunities available and the purposes underpinning the educative process. The question to ask in relation to gender is whether the educational process is about reproducing entrenched understandings of what it means to be a girl/woman, boy/man or whether education is the means for social and political change towards a gender equal society. This question becomes more complex when we look at the issue of gender and education in the global context of these international initiatives.

The connection between education, development and gender in the developing world is the basis of many initiatives – it is assumed that the more access to education girls and women will have the greater the range of benefits both for the girls/women individually as well as for the wider socio-political position of females. In the range of international initiatives under the overarching policy of *Education for All* education is seen as the key to improving both the material and cultural position of girls and women (UNICEF, 2005) as well as having a wider societal impact. In particular, longer education delays marriage and motherhood and so has an impact on population growth. Underpinning these ideas about the importance of education are though some significant tensions. There is an assumption that education is the route to both personal empowerment and the means to develop the agency of women. Though there exists a correlation between girls/women's education and low fertility, Jeffery and Jeffrey (1998) question whether this access to education necessarily enhances women's autonomy. There is an attractive logic: the longer the education, the later women enter into marriage and through education women can access wider opportunities including employment. However, the critical question concerns the underlying motivation both individually and politically for affording access to education. Is female education about the development of autonomy and citizenship or is it about increasing marriage prospects. Jeffery and Jeffrey argue that "women will not be empowered by their schooling if they remain embedded in structures that limit their room for manoeuvre. Clearly schooling may indeed empower women in some contexts but the educational provision and the forms of domestic organisation and the quality of education impact on women's autonomy" (p 249-50).

Fundamentally then, we need to look at the ideologies of gender underpinning the educative process: the construction of what it means to be a woman. From Jeffrey and Jeffrey's analysis we can see that hegemonic ideologies of femininity have accommodated ideas about female education to sustain rather than challenge the patriarchal social structure – a thread we have followed since Astell's (1692) proposal. Muito (2004) gives testimony to the underpinning gender issues in Kenyan education, for example, in terms of teacher expectations, sexist and sometimes abusive behaviour towards girls and the lowering of self esteem, all of which reinforce rather than challenge patriarchal gender relations. Further, Muito illustrates how backlash politics are impacting on efforts to improve the educational opportunities and experiences of girls, citing the development of arguments that there has been undue emphasis on girls' education in Kenya leading to the perception that boys are feeling 'left out'. Therefore it seems that efforts to improve the educational opportunities of girls and women globally, within western countries as well as in developing countries must challenge patriarchal understandings of gender relations if such efforts are to not only improve the lives of individual girls and women but bring about the anticipated socio political change. Is the answer then to turn to the second approach to gender: that of creating a woman/girl-centric educative process?

FEMALE-CENTRED EDUCATION

If we translate Kristeva's second phase, the task becomes one of the reconstruction of the educative process so that it takes as a central concern the experiences of women and of other minority groups who historically have been marginalized. With the increased levels of educational access and achievement by women and girls and by the progress of women in the education professions, it might be argued that this ambition has been achieved. However, we have to consider the questions posed by these trends: what are the challenges posed by (1) the male exodus from the teaching profession and (2) the male disengagement with education as learners.

Riddell and Tett (2006), in their survey of the gender imbalance of the teaching profession in Scotland – which is typical of many countries – suggest that one of the issues in the feminisation of the teaching profession is that teaching is no longer a prestigious occupation especially where there are many more employment opportunities. What we are seeing is the familiar pattern of men moving out and taking up what might be more attractive and more lucrative options rather than being 'forced out'. Simplistic understandings of education as mothering can become alienating both of women and men, not only removing men from the educative process but confining women to what might be deemed in patriarchal ideologies 'gender appropriate' arenas. We need to look to the more expansive ideas of education as caring, based on the classic idea of the 'feminine' (Noddings 1984, 2002) as an area of involvement of both men and women. With the current gender trends in the education professions this is an ever more urgent issue but again we need to understand what the issues are and not become reductive in our thinking about the construction of gender.

We have to consider the wider socio political consequences of an increasingly female dominated profession: are we seeing on a much wider social setting an increasing gender divided world. In the 'caring professions' and even in religious ministry within some Christian denominations, are we seeing the opting out of men and a replaying of traditional gender divisions which align female and caring? At a societal level this is not balanced nor is it good for education. This gender imbalance in the teaching profession can only lead to the increased marginalisation of education both as a profession and as an area of social policy and practice which in turn will limit the realisation of genuine gender equality. We are at the point where we need to see education as an enterprise into which both women and men – as educators and learners participate fully.

One issue in particular has helped spotlight the issue of gender imbalances in teaching – that of male teachers and the education of boys. Here again we must be careful not to be reductive in our thinking by making a simplistic link between the diminishing numbers of male teachers in all sectors of school education and the disengagement from education by some groups of boys. The question of role models was one of a number of strategies designed to enable girls to become involved in what traditional were regarded as male arenas, for example, science and engineering. Role models are important in widening opportunities. With the increase in the number of female headed households, there is an absence of males in the domestic context side by side with the feminisation of the teacher profession, there are significant concerns about the lack of positive male role models for boys particularly given the pervasive images of aggressive hyperbolic masculinity dominating a media rich popular culture. We need to remain critical and interrogate the underpinning understandings of gender. Recent campaigns in England in the UK to attract more men into primary teaching are an example of policy and practice in which there are uncritical assumptions about gender. As Burn (2001) demonstrates in these campaigns, it is not solely that boys need male teachers but certain types of boys – white working class boys who are deemed problematic – who need certain types of males teachers: a stereotypical image of white heterosexual (football loving) male teacher. Here we see the valorisation of particular versions of masculinity and not a recognition of the significance of diversity in terms of other social factors such as class, race and sexuality that exists. As Mills (2000) cautions, we need to move beyond a simplistic idea of boys needing male teachers and explore more critically the gender dynamics within classrooms and within school settings thus highlighting questions about pedagogic practices and gender.

As we have seen earlier, arising from the Women's Liberation Movement and the subsequent growth of radical, woman-centred politics, one of the significant developments in the education of women and girls was the appreciation of the way in which gender might influence the way in which girls and women learn. There is a danger that this can lead to the perception that there are different and competing educational needs. In both the context of the classroom as well as on a wider educational front we are then faced with the dilemma of which set of needs to address. Further, as Raphael Reed (1999) points up, there are difficulties in using narrowly based gender appropriate approaches within a diverse educational setting:

> Models of how to work in an emancipatory way with girls do not easily transfer across the gender divide, and dilemmas created by working from a radical or feminist perspective with pupils whose masculine identities in school often manifest as domineering and disruptive illuminate some of the significant limitations of gender work in schools and unproblematised notions of critical pedagogy. At the same time, it highlights the need to move beyond the prescriptions of a rigid binary categorisation of experience and build links across the divide, reading against the grain of how things are supposed to be (Raphael Reed 1999, p106).

Within feminism discussions there has been a significant critique of any essentialist stance which would claim determined gender attributes in thinking and learning. What has emerged from this work, as I argued earlier are pedagogies that appreciate different positions learners might occupy both in the short term and the long term. Raphael Reed similarly argues that we need firstly, to recognize of the multiple positions occupied by boys (and girls) and, secondly, develop pedagogic practices which for boys "encourage the building of critical learning dialogues and the internalisation of self-control, as a challenge to masculinised forms of knowledge, learning and social interaction" (p 106). In this solution, though we have to be constantly wary of recognising gender differences without these differences being reduced patriarchal understandings of what it means to male and female. This dilemma leads us to consider the third possibility of a gender-free education suggested by Kristeva.

A GENDER-FREE EDUCATION

In Kristeva's terms the construction of a gender free sociopolitical order is the utopian ideal but as we have seen in this book, the realisation of this vision within the material world and within education seems almost as far as away today as it was in the early days of second wave feminism in the late 1960s. We face intense pressure about the exclusion of males within education at the same time as the proliferation of exaggerated forms of hegemonic femininity and masculinity. However, our exploration of feminist utopian thinking helps point up two issues: firstly, the necessity of gender in education being constructed as two mutually exclusive sets of needs and secondly, the paradox of gender.

We can question the seeming necessity of basing our understandings, policy and practices in relation to gender in education as two mutually exclusive sets of needs. This construction of gender only reinforces hegemonic ideologies of masculinity and femininity and thereby limits the opportunities and achievements of girls and women, boys and men who do not live up to the ideal version of what it means to be female/male. We have to recognise the paradox of gender as it is currently constructed: at on level gender should have no significance in educational opportunities available to an individual and in the shaping of the educational process and practices they are involved in. At the same time, we have to recognise the deep meaning of gender in a person's life and identity. If we ignore issues related to gender, there is always the risk that we degenerate back to the position of 'gender blind' educational policy and practices which historically have limited the educational opportunities and achievement of women and girls. Huston (1994) suggests a 'gender sensitive' approach where difference is not reductive to what girls/boys need or prefer but is aware of the ways in which gender can impact on identity and on educational progress. However, this construction of a 'gender-sensitive' approach may be insufficient in dealing with the complexities of identity and educational progress particularly in a global context. We need to move beyond the current bounded ideologies of gender – bounded in terms of historical understandings shaped by patriarchal sociopolitical systems – and instead move to future oriented understanding of gender and education in a dynamic global sociopolitical context. For this we can look to feminist utopian thinking which has challenged not only patriarchal ideologies of gender but questioned alternative constructions of what it means to be female or male in education. Central in these discussions has been the conceptualisation of identity not as bounded or as determined as current educational policy and practice would suggest.

Haraway (1990) sees "subjectivity structured around a multiple set of coordinates such as class, race, age and sexuality which all work together in the creation of identity" (p 27). We have to recognise not just the significance of gender but gender sits alongside other identities some of which might have more constancy than others but are critical to the experience and achievements of individuals in education: social class, race, sexuality all impact on the educational experiences of individuals. But other more fluid identities are equally important, identities as a learner (Head, forthcoming) or as a teacher all become important in shaping educational experience.

While there is an attractiveness in the figure of the cyborg and it does help to disrupt ideas about unitary subjectivity, Sunden (2001) asks, whether "discursive transformations in narratives in itself lead to material transformations and social change" (p 217). The critical question is whether the figure of the cyborg remains on the periphery of the symbolic order rather than act as a lever for change? For Haraway critically important in the disruption of unquestioned assumptions is the telling of stories to envision alternatives to the dominant ideologies. These narratives of the marginalized allow not only a space to consider alternative possibilities but also afford the possibility of sociopolitical change around issues related to gender.

There is an increasing body of thought and political activism around 'global feminism'. Global feminism can be defined in the development of debates and political activism related to the position of women in a context of globalised advanced capitalism. This body of work looks at the core concerns in relation to the position of women in terms of access to social and health services, to education, their legal position including that in the family, their representation politically. However, this work is not simply a replaying of the demands of western feminism. Instead, this work is concerned with the position of women in very different contexts and is concerned with a range such as the environment, the role of transnational corporations, the spread of disease including pandemics such as the Aids crises in many countries around the world. The slogan 'think locally, act globally' (Kerr, 2004) sums up a central idea underpinning a global feminist politics: at every stage of political action or analysis there is a need to look for local impact but also to be concerned about the global context. I would add another dimension to this in that in the formulation of feminist utopian thinking we also have a future orientation which allows us to consider what kind of society are we seeking to create by today's actions. These actions do not have to be shaped by deterministic understandings of gender where the differential positions of women and men are held as natural. Feminist utopian thinking provides the opportunity for the formulation of 'not-yet-conscious' ideas (Block, 1986) and underpin policy and practice in education with hope – whether this is 'robust hope' (Sawyer, 2006) or 'ultimate hope' (Halpin, 2003) of the possibility of change in terms of gender relations.

In feminist utopian thinking, the 'good society' is not a determined utopia is the classic sense of a perfect and stable society but is more about a dynamic society constantly grappling with issues of fairness and equality. Symington and Sprenger (2004) look to the year 2033 and provide a vision of a transformed society, the outcome of feminist politics. The vision is not fully formed and indeed is part dystopian and part eutopian but what this vision exemplifies it the importance of feminist utopian thinking in seeking solutions to 'the gender problem' in education: that to seek a simplistic answer only leads to the situation in which the needs of girls/women are set in competition to those of boys/men. Seeking solutions is a dynamic process in which the paradox of gender – being one and the same time both deeply meaningful and at the same having no significance on educational achievement – is grappled with.

> The year is 2033…
> Three decades into this new millennium, we find ourselves on a transformed planet. Over the last thirty years the world has changed substantially, in terms of the environment and climate, populations, geopolitics and socioeconomic levels. Who would have known, that water – not oil – would become the most sought-after commodity in the world
>
> […]
>
> There have been significant achievements in medical science with cures found for major diseases like HIV/AIDS but this is a double edged sword with reproductive technologies to produce the 'ideal' children – blue eyed and pale skinned – and cloning has been used to replicate the 'ideal' woman – "a nimble fingered woman who needs very little sleep" (p 1). Patriarchal notions of what it means to be a woman are still recycled through religions and beliefs. Nevertheless, there have been laudable achievements as well as major setbacks. The struggle has not been an easy one, but women's movements have indeed shaped the world we now live in. Feminist leaders have formed powerful political parties, moved into key positions in all international institutions, and have been able to define, debate and broadcast the new 'spirituality' based on universal human rights – irrespective of sex, religion, caste, class sexuality, ability or race. Feminist forged alliances across all identities and social movements. We built political and economic agendas that the majority of government departments, international institutions and businesses could no longer. We fought back from the local level right up to the World Trade Organization to ensure that every woman, man and child had clean and accessible water, adequate shelter and a nutritious diet. With heart, soul, humour, passion, wisdom and energy, women's rights have been defined and defended across this planet. We continue to be leaders in movements to advance the equal rights of all as ever new challenges arise (p 1-2).

Here, to my mind, the visionary quality of feminism is evident. The vision is very much about not an ideal but an improved socio-political order in which we continue to grapple with the utopian idea of the process of social change towards the better society and the critical interrogation of the process and the underpinning ideologies. These aspects reinforce education as a process of both human formation and of social and political transformation to achieve the better society.

With writings on global feminism the focus is not on image and self representation but instead the development of visions and strategies to bring about social change within a globalised context. In this we see an evolution of the arguments about differences in the 1990s. There is still as Symington and Sprenger (2004) note a strong commitment to collective action, to basis political action on the improvement of the position of women and girls in society but a more developed sense of the complexities involved. The critical question for them is to develop a common politics where there are significant differences in the lived experience of different groups of women globally:

> How can we remain committed to collective action to improve the status of women, yet reject simple solutions and universal assumptions that will not help to bring our visions of a just future to fruition?" (p 13).

BIBLIOGRAPHY

Albinski, N. B. (1988) *Women's Utopias in British and American Fiction*, London: Routledge.

Allen, P. (1973) 'Free Space' in Koedt, A., Levine, E. and Rapone, A. (Eds.) *Radical Feminism*, New York: Quadrangle Books, 271-279.

Alpert, J. (1974) *Mother Right: A New Feminist Theory* from http://scriptorium.lib.duke.edu/wlm/mother/ (accessed 22nd Dec 2006).

Arditti, R., Klein, R.D. and Minden, S. (1989) (Eds.) *Test-Tube Women: What Future for Motherhood?* London: Pandora Press.

Arnold, J. (1995) *The Cook and The Carpenter*, New York: New York University Press.

Arnold, J. (2000) 'Consciousness-Raising' in Crow, B.A. (Ed.) *Radical Feminism: A Documentary Reader*, New York: New York University Press, 282-286.

As, B. (1989) 'The Feminist University' in Klein, R.D. and Steinberg, D.L. (Eds.) *Radical Voices: A Decade of Feminist Resistance from Women's International Forum*, Oxford: Pergammon Press, 192-198.

Astell, M. (1986) 'A Serious Proposal to the Ladies' in Hill. B. (Ed.) *The First English Feminist: Reflections Upon Marriage and Other Writings By Mary Astell,* Aldershot, Hants, Gower/Maurice Temple Smith, 135-182 (1st published 1694).

Astell, M. (1997) 'A Serious Proposal to the Ladies Part II' in Springborg, P. (Ed.) *Mary Astell: A Serious Proposal to the Ladies Part I and Part II*, London: Pickering and Chatto, 67-196 (1st published 1697).

Atwood, M. (1987) *The Handmaid's Tale*, London: Jonathan Cape.

Atwood, M. (2005) 'Writing Utopia' in Atwood, M. (Ed.) *Curious Pursuits: Occasional Writing*, London: Virago.

Balsamo, A. (1995) 'Forms of Technological Embodiment: Reading the Body in Contemporary Culture' in Featherstone, M. and Burrows, R. (Eds.) *Cyberspace, Cyberbodies, Cyberpunk. Cultures of Technological Embodiment*, London: Sage, 215-237.

Bammer, A. (1991) *Partial Visions: Feminism and Utopianism in the 1970s*, New York: Routledge.

Barr, M. (1987) *Alien To Femininity: Speculative Fiction and Feminist Theory*, Westport, Connecticut: Greenwood Press,

Barr, M. (1990) ''Men in Feminist Science Fiction: Marge Piercy, Thomas Berger and the End of Masculinity' in Garnett, R and Ellis, R. J. (Eds.) *Science Fiction Roots and Branches: Contemporary Critical Approaches*, New York: Macmillan/St. Martin's, 153-167.

Barr, M (1992) *Feminist Fabulation: Space/Postmodern Fiction*, Iowa City: University of Iowa Press.

Barr, M (1993) *Lost in Space: Probing Feminist Science Fiction and Beyond*, Chapel Hill, North Carolina: The University of North Carolina Press.

Bartkowski, F. (1989) *Feminist Utopias*, Lincoln, Nebraska: University of Nebraska Press.

Baumgarder, J. and Richards, A. (2000) *ManifestA: young women, feminism and the future*, New York: Farrar, Straus and Giroux.

BBC (2006) *Blair to tackle menace children*, BBC interview, 2006/08/31 18:01:19 GMT from http://news.bbc.co.uk/go/pr/fr/-/1/hi/uk_politics/5301824.stm (accessed 1st November 2006)

Beck, U. (1997) *The Reinvention of Politics: Rethinking Modernity in the Global Social Order*, Cambridge: Polity Press.

Belenky, M., Clinchy, B., Goldberger, N. and Tarule, J. (1986) *Wome's Ways of Knowing: The Development of Self, Voice and Mind*, USA: Basic Books.

Bell, S. Morrow, M. and Tastsoglou, E. (1999) 'Teaching in Environments of Resistance: Towards a Critical Feminist and Anti Racist Pedagogy' in Mayberry, M. and Rose, E. (Eds.) *Meeting the Challenge: Innovative Feminist Pedagogies on Action*, New York and London: Routledge, 23-46.

Bellamy, E. (1982) *Looking Backwards*, Harmondsworth, Middlesex: Penguin Books.

Bernard, J. (1975) *The Future of Parenthood: The New Role of Mothers*, London: Calder and Boyers.

Bloch, E. (1986) *The Principle of Hope*, Oxford: Basil Blackwell (trans. Plaice, N. Plaice, S. and Knight, P.)

Bonin, E. L. (2000) 'Margaret Cavendish's Dramatic Utopias and the Politics of Gender' in *Studies in English Literature* 40(2) 339-354.

Bornstein, C. (2005) 'Representing The Third Wave: Mainstream Print Media Framing A New Feminist Movement', in *Journalism and Mass Communication* Quarterly, 82(4), 783-803.

Bornstein, K. (1994) *Gender Outlaw: On Men, Women and the Rest of Us*, New York/London: Routledge.

Bowlby, J. (1969) *Attachment and Loss: 1 Attachment*, London: Hogarth Press.

Bowles, G. (1980) 'Is Women's Studies an Academic Discipline?' in G. Bowles and R.D. Klien (Eds.) *Theories of Women's Studies*, London: Routledge Kegan and Paul 32-45.

Braidotti, R (1996) *Cyberfeminism with a Difference*, from http://www.let.uu.nl/~Rosi.Braidotti/personal/articles.html (accessed 12th November 2006)

Brownmiller, S. *Femininity*, New York: Simon and Schuster, 1984.

Burdekin, K. (1937) (Pseud. Constantine, M.) *Swastika Nights*, London: Victor Gollancz, 1937.

Burgess, A. (1997) *Fatherhood Reclaimed: The Making of The Modern Father*, London: Vermillion.

Burn, E. (2001) *Do Boys Need Teachers as Positive Role Models?* Paper presented at the British Educational Research Association Annual Conference, Leeds University, 13-15 September 2001, from http://www.leeds.ac.uk/educol/documents/00001884.htm (accessed 11th Nov 2006).

Burris, B. (1973) 'The Fourth World Manifesto' in Koedt, A., Levine, E. and Rapone, A. (Eds.) *Radical Feminism*, New York: Quadrangle Books, 323-357.

Burwell, J. (1997) *Notes on Nowhere: Feminism, Utopian Logic and Social Transformation*, Minneapolis, USA: University of Minneapolis Press.

Butler, J. (1990) *Gender Trouble. Feminism and the Subversion of Identity*, London: Routledge.

Butler, J. (1993) *Bodies That Matter: On the Discursive Limitations of "Sex"*, New York/London: Routledge.

Butler, M. and Todd, J. (1989) (Eds.) *The Works of Mary Wollstonecraft*, London: William Pickering.

Callenbach, E. (1975) *Ecotopia: The Notebooks and Reports of William Weston*, London/New York: Bantam Books.

Camp, L. J. (1996) 'We are Geeks and We are not Guys': The Systers Mailing List' in Cherny, L. and Weise, E. R. (Eds.) *Wired_Women: Gender and New Realities in Cyberspace*, Seattle: Seal Press.

Cavendish, M. (1992) 'A Description of a New World Called Blazing World', in Lilley, K. (Ed.) *A description of a new world called Blazing World*, London: Pickering.

Chapone, H. (1996) 'Letters on the Improvement of the Mind 1773' in Todd, J. (Ed.) *Female Education in the Age of Enlightenment*, Vol. 2 London: William Pickering.

Charlton, K. (2002) 'Women and Education' in Pacheco, A. (Ed.) *A Companion to Early Modern Women's Writing*, Oxford: Blackwell.

Charnas, S. McKee. (1989) *Walk to the End of the World*, London: The Women's Press.

Charnas, S. McKee. (1989) *Motherlines*, London: The Women's Press.

Chicago Women's Liberation Union (1971) *How to Start Your Own Consciousness-Raising Group*, from, http://www.Cwluherstory.Com?Cwluarchive/Crcwlu.html (accessed 5th May 2006).

Chodorow, N. (1978) *The Reproduction of Mothering: Psychoanalysis and the Sociology of Gender*, Berkeley/London: University of California Press.

Cixous, H. (1981) 'The Laugh of the Medusa' in Marks, E. and I. De Courtrivon, *New French Feminisms*, Hemel Hempstead: Harvester Wheatsheaf, 245 -264.

Coffey, A. and Delamont, S. (2000) *Feminism and the Classroom Teacher: Research, Praxis and Pedagogy*, London/New York: Routledge Falmer.

Collins, P. H. (1990) *Black Feminist Thought: Knowledge, Consciousness and the Politics of Empowerment*, New York/London.

Combahee River Collective (1998) 'A Black Feminist Statement' in Nardi, P. M. and B. E. Schneider (Eds.) *Social Perspectives in Lesbian and Gay Studies*, London: Routledge, 521-526 (originally drafted 1977).

Connell, R. W. (2000) *The Men and the Boys*, Cambridge: Polity Press.

Cook, A. and Kirk, G. (1983) (Eds.) *Greenham Women Everywhere Dreams, Ideas and Actions from the Women's Peace Movement*, London: Pluto 1983.

Coyner, S. (1983) 'Women's Studies as an Academic Discipline: Why and How to Do It', in G. Bowles and R. D. Klien (Eds.) *Theories of Women's Studies*, London: Routledge Kegan and Paul, 46-71.

Cream, J. (1991) 'Resolving Riddles: The Sexed Body' in Bell, D. and Valentine, G. (Eds.) *Mapping Desire: Geographies of Sexualities*, London/New York: Routledge, 31-40.

Daly, M. (1980) *Beyond God the Father: Towards a Philosophy of Women's Liberation*, London: The Women's Press.

Daly, M. (1979) *Gyn/Ecology: The Metaethics of Radical Feminism*, London: The Women's Press.

Davis, R. (2006) 'Education, Utopia and the Limits of the enlightenment' in Peters, M. and Moir-Freeman, J. (Eds.) *Edutopias: New Utopian Thinking in Education*, Rotterdam: Sense Publishers, 125-143.

De Beauvoir, S. (1977) *The Second Sex*, Harmondsworth, Middlesex: Penguin Books.

Delaney, S. (1992) *Triton*, London: Grafton.

Dewey, J. (1933) 'Dewey Outlines Utopian Schools' in Boydston, J.A. (Ed.) *John Dewey: The Later Works*. Vol. 9, 1933-1934. South Illinois University Press: Carbondale and Edwardsville, 136-140.

Dewey, J. (1966) *Democracy and Education: An Introduction to the Philosophy of Education*, London: Collier-Macmillan

Dixie, Lady F. (1890) *Gloriana or the Revolution of 1900*, London: Henry.

Doherty, W. J. (1997) 'The Best of Times and the Worst of Times: Fathering as a Contested Arena of Academic Discourse' in Hawkins, A.J. and Dollahite (1997) (Eds.) *Generative Fathering: Beyond Deficit Perspectives*, Thousand Oaks, California: Sage, 217-227.

Donovan, J. (1992) *Feminist Theory: The Intellectual Traditions of American Feminism*, New York: Continuum, 2nd ed.

Dworkin, A. 'Our Blood: The Slavery of Women in Amerika' in Dworkin, A. *Our Blood: Prophecies and Discourses on Sexual Politics*, London: The Women's Press, 76-95.

Eagleton, M. (2003) 'Re-Reading the Seventies: Re-Reading Women's Silence' in Graham, H., Kaloski, A. Neilson, A and Robertson, E. (Eds.) *The Feminist Seventies*, York: Raw Nerve Press, 109-120.

Eisenstein, H. (1984) *Contemporary Feminist Thought*, London: Unwin.

Erikson, E. H. (1964) *Childhood and Society*, New York; Norton, 2nd ed.

Escobar, A. (1999) 'Gender, Place and Networks. A Political Ecology of Cyberculture' in Harcourt, W. (Ed.) *Women @ Internet: Creating New Cultures in Cyberspace*, London: Zed Books, 31-58.

Espstein, J. and Straub, K. (Eds.) (1991) *Body Guards*, New York: Routledge.

Faderman, L. (1992) *Odd Girls and Twilight Lovers: A History of Lesbian Life in Twentieth Century America*, Harmondsworth, Middlesex: Penguin Book.

Faludi, S. (1992) *Backlash: The Undeclared War Against Women*, London: Chatto and Windus.

Featherstone, M. and Burrows, R. (1995) 'Cultures of Technological Embodiment: An Introduction' in Featherstone, M. and Burrows, R. (Eds.) *Cyberspace, Cyberbodies, Cyberpunk. Cultures of Technological Embodiment*, London: Sage, 1-20.

Feminist Anthology Collective (1981) *No Turning Back: Writings from the Women's Liberation Movement 1975-1980*, London: The Women's Press.

Finden, B. (1995) (Ed.) *Listen Up: Voices from the Next Generation*, Seattle: Seal Press.

Firestone, S. (1979) *The Dialectic of Sex*, London: The Women's Press.

Fordyce, J. (1766) 'Sermon VIII on Female Virtue with Intellectual Accomplishments: Sermons for Young Women', in Todd, J. (1996) (Ed.) *Female Education in the Age of Enlightment Vol. 1*, London: William Pickering.

Foucault, M. (1984) 'Of Other Spaces' in *Architecture/Mouvement/Continuitie (Des Espace Autres* 1967, trans, Miskowiec, J.) from http://www.foucault.info/documents/heteroTopia/foucault.heteroTopia.en.html (accessed 8th November 2006).

Freeman, J. (1975) *The Politics of Women's Liberation*, New York: Policy Press.

Freeman, J. (2004) *Trends in Education Equity of Girls and Women 2004,* National Center for Educational Statistics, Washington, US: US Department of Education

Freud, S. (1977a) 'Some Psychical Consequences of the Anatomical Distinction between The Sexes' in Freud, S., *On Sexuality: Three Essays on the Theory of Sexuality and Other Works,* Harmondsworth, Middlesex: Penguin Books. 1977a, 331-334.

Freud, S. (1977b) 'Female Sexuality' in Freud, S. *On Sexuality: Three Essays on the Theory of Sexuality and Other Works*, Harmondsworth, Middlesex: Penguin Books, 371-392.

Friere, P. (1972) *Pedagogy of the Oppressed*, Harmondsworth, Middlesex: Penguin (trans. Ramos, M.B.)

Frye, N. (1973) 'Varieties of Literary Utopias' in Manuel, F. (Ed.) *Utopias and Utopian Thought,* London: Souvenir Press, 323-347.

Fuss, D. (1989) *Speaking. Feminism, Nature and Difference*, Routledge: London.

Gearhart, S. M. (1979) *The Wanderground*, London: The Women's Press.

Gearhart, S. M. (1984) 'Future Visions: Today's Politics: Feminist Utopias in Review' in Rohrlich, R. and Baruch, E. H. (Eds.) *Women in Search of Utopias: Mavericks and Mythmakers,* New York: Schocken Books, 296-309.

Gibson, W. (1995) *Neuromancer,* London: Harpercollins.

Giddens, A. (1994) *Beyond Left and Right: The Future of Radical Politics*, Cambridge: Polity Press.

Giddens, A. (1998) *The Third Way: The Renewal of Social Democracy*, Cambridge: Polity Press.

Gill, R. (2000) 'Review' in *Feminist Review*, 64, 139-143.

Gilligan, C. (1982) *In a Different Voice: Psychological Theory and Women's Development*, Cambridge, Mass, London: Harvard University Press

Gillis, S. and Munford, R. (2004) 'Genealogies and Generations: The Political and Praxis of Third Wave Feminism' in *Women's History Review* 13(2) 165-182.

Gilman, C. P. (1979) *Herland*, London: The Women's Press.

Godfrey, J. J. (1987) *A Philosophy of Human Hope*, Dordrecht, The Netherlands, Martinus Nijhoff.

Gom, L. (1993) *The Y Chromosome*, Toronto: Second Story Press.

Goodman, R. T. (2004) *World, Class, Women: Global Literature, Education and Feminism,* London & New York: Routledge Falmer.

Gramsci, A. (1971) *Selections from Prison Notebooks*, London: Lawrence Wishart.

Gregory, J. (1774) 'A Father's Legacy to His Daughters', in Todd, J. (1996) (Ed.) *Female Education in the Age of Enlightenment*, Vol. 1, William Pickering: London.

Griffith, A. I. and Smith, D. E. (2005) *Mothering for Schooling*. New York and London: Routledge Falmer.

Griswold, R. (1997) 'Generative Fathering: A Historical Perspective' in Hawkins, A. J. and Dollahite, D. (1997) (Eds.) *Generative Fathering: Beyond Deficit Perspectives*, Thousand Oaks, California: Sage, 71-86.

Grosz, E. (1990) 'Contemporary Theories of Power and Subjectivity' in Gunew, S. (Ed.) *Feminist Knowledge: Critique and Construct,* London: Routledge, 59-120.

Gunew, S. (1990) 'Feminist Knowledge: Critique and Construct' in Gunew, S. (Ed.) *Feminist Knowledge: Critique and Construct*. London: Routledge, 13-35.

Gunther-Canada, W. (2001) *Rebel Writer: Mary Wollstonecraft and Enlightenment Politics,* DeKalb Illinois: Northern Illinois Press.

Gurian, M. and Henley, P. (2001) *Boys and Girls Learn Differently! A Guide to Teachers and Parents*, San Francisco, California: Jossey-Bass.

Halbert, D. (2004) 'Shulamith Firestone: Radical Feminism and Visions of the Information Society', in *Information, Communication and Society*, 7(1) 115-135.

Halpin, D. (2001) 'The Nature of Hope and Its Significance for Education', in *British Journal of Educational Studies*, 4(4) 392-410.
Halpin, D. (2003a) *Hope and Education: The Role of the Utopian Imagination*, London: Routledge Falmer.
Halpin, D. (2003b) *London Lives and Education*. London: Institute of Education, University of London.
Hanisch, C. (2000) 'The Personal is Political' in Crow, B. A. (Ed.) *Radical Feminism: A Documentary Reader*, New York: New York University Press, 113-116.
Haraway, D. (1990) 'A Manifesto for Cyborgs: Science, Technology, and Socialist Feminism in the 1980s' in Nicholson, L. (Ed.) *Feminism/Post Modernism*, London: Routledge, 190-233.
Haraway, D. (1997) *Modest – Witness@ Second – Millennium. Femaleman©-Meets -Oncomouse™: Feminism and Technoscience*, London: Routledge.
Harrison, J. (1968) 'Introduction' in Harrison. J. (Ed.) *Utopianism and Education: Robert Owen and the Owenites*, New York: Teachers College Press.
Hawkins, A. J. and Dollahite, D. (1997) *Generative Fathering: Beyond Deficit Perspectives*, Thousand Oaks, California: Sage.
Hawthorne, S. and Klien, R. (1999) 'Cyberfeminism' in Hawthorne, S and Klein, R. (Eds.) *Cyber-feminisms Connectivity, Critique and Creativity*, Australia: Spinifex.
Heilbrun, C. (1973) *Towards Androgyny: Aspects of Male and Female in Literature*, London: Victor Gollancz.
Heywood, L. and Drake, J. (1997) (Eds.) *Third Wave Agenda: Being Feminist, Doing Feminist*, Minneapolis: University of Minnesota.
Hill. B. (Ed.) (1986) 'Introduction' in *The First English Feminist: Reflections Upon Marriage and Other Writings by Mary Astell*, Aldershot, Hants. Gower/Maurice Temple Smith, 1-62.
Hobby, E. (1988) *Virtue of Necessity*: English Women's Writing 1646-1688, London: Virago.
Hogeland, L. M. (1998) *Feminism and its Fictions: The Consciousness-Raising Novel and the Women's Liberation Movement*, Philadelphia: University of Pennsylvania Press.
hooks, b. (1982) *Ain't I a Woman: Black Women and Feminism*, London/Winchester Mass.: Pluto Press.
hooks, b. (1984) *Feminist Theory: From Margin to Center*, USA: South End Press.
hooks, b. (1994) *Teaching to Transgress: Education as the Practice of Freedom*, London & New York: Routledge.
Howe, C. (1997) *Gender and Classroom Interaction: A Research Review*, Edinburgh: SCRE.
Hull, G., Scott, P. B and Smith. B. (Eds.) (1982) *But Some of Us Are Brave*, Old Westbury, New York: Feminist Press.
Houston, B. (1994) 'Should Public Education be Gender-Free?' in Stone, L. (Ed.) *The Education Feminism Reader*, New York & London: Routledge.
Huxley, A. (1976) *Brave New World*, Harmondsworth, Middlesex: Penguin Books.
Irigaray L. (1985) 'This Sex Which Is Not One' in Irigaray L. *This Sex Which Is Not One*, Ithaca, New York: Cornell University Press (trans. Porter, C. First Published *As Ce Sexe Qui N'en Pas Un*, Paris: Editions De Minuit, 1977).
Jackson, S. (2004) *Differently Academic?Developing Lifelong Learning for Women in Higher Education*, Dordecht/London: Kluwer Academic Publishers.
Jaggar, A. M. (1983) *Feminist Politics and Human Nature*, Sussex: Harvester Press.
Jameson, F. (1982) 'Progress Versus Utopia; Or, Can We Imagine the Future?' in *Science Fiction Studies*, 9 (2) 147-58.
Jameson, F. (2005) *Archaeologies of the Future*, London: Verso.
Jeffrey, P. and Jeffrey, R. (1998) 'Silver Bullet or Passing Fancy? Girls' Schooling and Population Policy in Jackson, C. and Pearson, R. (Eds.) *Feminist Visions of Development: Gender Analysis and Policy*, London and New York: Routledge.
Jones, A. I. and Merchant, E. (1991) *Unveiling a Parallel*, Syracuse, New York: Syracuse University Press (1st published 1893).
Kane, J. (2006) 'School exclusions and masculine, working class identities' in *Gender and Education*, 18(6) 673-685.

Kanter, H., LeFanu, S., Shah, S. and Spedding, C. (Eds.) (1984) *Sweeping Statements: Writings from the Women's Liberation Movement 1981-83,* London: The Women's Press.

Kelly, G. (Ed.) (1999) 'Introduction to A Description of Millennium Hall' in Kelly, G. (Ed.) *Millennium Hall*, Peterborough, Ontario: Broadview Press.

Kerr, J., Sprenger, E. and Symington, A. (Eds.) (2004) *The Future of Women's Rights*, London/New York: Zed Books.

Kenway, J. (2004) *Gender Reforms in Schools: Slip-Sliding Away*, Conference Paper for Our A(gender): Demanding Equality, Australian Education Union Women's Conference, Melbourne Australia 2 & 3 Oct.

Kessler, C. F. (Ed.) (1984) *Daring to Dream: Utopian Stories by United States Women 1836-1919*, Boston: Pandora.

Kitch, S. (2000) *Higher Ground: From Utopianism to Realism in Feminist Thought and Theory*, Chicago: Chicago University Press.

Klein, T. J. (1989) 'Teaching and Mother Love' in *Educational Theory* 39(4), 373-383.

Kohlberg, L (1981) *The Philosophy of Moral Judgement and the Idea of Justice*, San Francisco: Harper Row.

Kolmerten, C. (1998) *Women in Utopia: The Ideology of Gender in American Owenite Communities*, Syracuse, New York: Syracuse University Press.

Koonz, C. (1988) *Motherhood in the Fatherland: the Family and Nazi Politics*, London: Methuen.

Kristeva, J. (1991) 'Woman's Time' in Warhol, R. R. and Price Hernal, D. (Eds.) *Feminisms: An Anthology of Literary Theory and Criticism*. New Brunswick, New Jersey: Rutgers University Press, 443-462.

Kumar, K. (1987) *Utopia and Anti-Utopia in Modern Times*, Oxford: Basil Blackwell.

Lane, A. J. (1979) 'Introduction' in Gilman, C.P. (1979) *Herland,* London: The Women's Press.

Laquer, T. (1990) *Making Sex: Body and Gender from the Greeks to Freud*, Cambridge, Mass.: Harvard University Press.

Levitas, R. (1990) *The Concept of Utopia*, Hemel Hempstead, Herts. Phillip Allan.

Levitas, R. (2004) 'Hope and Education: Review Article' in *Journal of Philosophy of Education* 38 (2), 269-273.

Lewis, M. (1990) 'Interrupting Patriarchy: politics, resistance and transformation in the feminist classroom' in *Harvard Educational Review* 60 (4), 467-488

Lilley, K. (1992) 'Blazing Worlds: Seventeenth-Century Women's Utopian Writing' in Brant, C. and Purkiss, D. (Eds.) *Woman, Texts and Histories 1575-1760*, London: Routledge 102-133.

Locke, J. (1996) *Some thoughts concerning education; and of the conduct of the understanding*, Cambridge: Hackett.

Lorde, A. (1984) 'The Master's Tools Will Never Dismantle the Master's House' in Lorde, A. *Sister Outsider, The Audrey Lorde Compendium*, London: Pandora, 158-161.

Macaulay, C. (1790) 'Letters On Education', in Todd, J. (1996) (Ed.) *Female Education in the Age of Enlightment*, Vol. 1, London: William Pickering.

MacKinnon, C. A. (1989) *Towards a Feminist Theory of State,* Cambridge, Mass. USA: Harvard University Press.

Maher, F. A. and Tetreault, M. K. T. (1994) *The Feminist Classroom*, New York: Basic Books.

Makin, B. (1980) *An Essay to Revive the Antient Education of Gentlewomen 1673*, Los Angeles, University of California, The Augustan Reprint Society No 202.

Malak, A. (1987) ''Margaret Atwood's The Handmaid's Tale and The Dystopian Tradition' in *Canadian Literature* 112, 9-16.

Mannheim, K. (1954) *Ideology and Utopia: An Introduction to the Sociology of Knowledge*, London: Routledge & Kegan Paul.

Manuel, F. E. and Manuel, F. P. (1979) *Utopian Thought in the Western World*, Oxford: Basil Blackwell.

Marcel, G. (1951) *Homo Viator: Introduction to a Metaphysics of Hope,* London: Victor Gollancz.

Marcuse, H. (1966) *Eros and Civilisation*, Boston: The Beacon Press, 2nd ed.
Marcuse, H. (1970) 'The End of Utopia' in Marcuse, H. Five Lectures: *Psychoanalysis, Politics and Utopia*, Boston: The Beacon Press, 62-82.
Mayberry, M. (1999) 'Reproductive and Resistant Pedagogies: The Comparative Roles of Collaborative Learning and Feminist Pedagogy in Science Education' in Mayberry, M. and Rose. E. (Eds.) *Meeting the Challenge: Innovative Feminist Pedagogies in Action*, New York and London: Routledge, 1-22.
Mazumdar, P. (1992) *Eugenics, Human Genetics and Human Failings: The Eugenics Society, Its Sources and Its Critics in Britain*, London: Routledge.
Mc Carron, K. (1995) 'Corpses, Animals, Machines and Mannequins: The Body and Cyberpunk' in Featherstone, M. and Burrows, R. (Eds.) *Cyberspace, Cyberbodies, Cyberpunk. Cultures of Technological Embodiment*. London: Sage, 261-273.
McKenna, E. (2001) *The Task of Utopia*, Lanham, Maryland: Rowan and Littlefield.
Mellor, A. (2002) 'Mary Wollstonecraft's A Vindication of the Rights of Women and The Women Writers of Her Day' in Johnson, C. (Ed.) *The Cambridge Companion to Mary Wollstonecraft*, Cambridge: Cambridge University Press, 24-41.
Midgley, M. (1996) *Utopias, Dolphins and Computers: Problems of Philosophical Plumbing*, London: Routledge.
Miller, J. B. (1986) *Toward a New Psychology of Women*, London: Pelican Books, 2nd ed.
Mills, M. (2000) 'Issues in implementing boys' programme in schools: male teachers and empowerment' in *Gender and Education*, 12 (2), 221-238.
Milojevic, I. (2005) *Educational Futures: Dominant and Contesting Visions*, London: Routledge.
Mitchell, J. (1990) *Psychoanalysis and Feminism: A Radical Reassessment of Freudian Psychoanalysis*, Harmondsworth, Middlesex: Penguin.
More, T. (1967) *Utopia*. Harmondsworth, Middlesex: Penguin Books (trans. Paul Turner).
Moraga, C. and Anzaldua, G. (Eds.) (1983) *This Bridge Called My Back: Writings by Radical Women of Colour*, New York: Kitchen Table Press.
Moylan, T. (1986) *Demand the Impossible: Science Fiction and the Utopian Imagination*, London/New York: Methuen, 1986.
Moylan, T. (2000) *Scraps of the Untainted Sky: Science Fiction, Utopia, Dystopia*, Boulder, Colorado: Westview.
Muito, M. (2004) *Gender Equality in the Classroom: "Reflections on Practice"*, Paper prepared Gender, Education and Development project Seminar on Pedagogic Strategies for Gender Equality and Quality Basic Education in Schools, Nairobi, Kenya 2nd February 2004, http://k1.ioe.ac.uk/schools/efps/GenderEducDev/Muito%20paper.pdf (accessed 11th November 2006).
Neill, A. S. (1962) *Summerhill*, Harmondsworth, Middlesex: Penguin.
Nixon, N. (1999) 'Cyberpunk: Preparing the Ground for Revolution or Keeping the Boys Satisfied', in Wolmark, J. (Ed.) *Cybersexualities; A Reader on Feminist Theory, Cyborgs and Cyberspace*, Edinburgh: Edinburgh University Press, 191-207.
Noddings, N. (1984) *Caring: A Feminine Approach to Ethics and Moral Education*, Berkeley, Los Angles: University of California Press.
Noddings, N. (1988) 'An Ethic of Caring and its Implications for Instructional Arrangements' in *American Journal of Education*, 96(2) 215-230.
Noddings, N. (2002) *Educating Moral People: A Caring Alternative to Character Education*, New York: Teachers College Press.
Nozick, R. (1974) *Anarchy, State and Utopia*, Oxford: Blackwell.
Okin, S. M. (1980) *Women in Western Political Thought*, London: Virago.
Orwell, G. (1990) *Nineteen Eighty Four*, Harmondsworth, Middlesex: Penguin.
Owen, R. (1968) 'A New Vision of Society' in Harrison. J. (Ed.) *Utopianism and Education: Robert Owen and the Owenites*, New York: Teachers College Press.

Peter, K. and Horn, L. (2005) *Gender Differences in Participation and Completion of Undergraduate Education and How They Have Changed over Time: Postsecondary Education Descriptive Analysis Reports*. Washington, US: US Department of Education.

Peters, M. and Freeman-Moir, J. (2006) 'Introducing Edutopias; Concept, Genealogy and Futures', in Peters, M. and Moir-Freeman, J. (Eds.) *Edutopias: New Utopian Thinking in Education*, Rotterdam: Sense Publishers, 1-20.

Perry, B. (1986) *The Celebrated Mary Astell: An Early English Feminist*, Chicago and London: The University of Chicago.

Perry, W. G. (1970) *Forms of Intellectual and Ethical Development in the College Years*, New York: Holt, Rinehart & Winston.

Phoenix, A., Woollett, A. and Lloyd, E. (Eds.) (1991) *Motherhood: Meanings, Practices and Ideologies*, London: Sage.

Piercy, M. and Freeman, J. (1972) *Getting Together: A Pamphlet by Cape Cod Women's Liberation*, from http://Research.Umbc.Edu/~Korenman/Wmst/Crguide2.html (accessed 5th May 2006).

Piercy, M. (1970) 'The Grand Coolie Damn' in Morgan, R. (Ed.) *Sisterhood Is Powerful*, New York: Vintage Books, 421-438.

Piercy, M. (1979) *Woman on the Edge of Time*, London: The Women's Press.

Piercy, M. (1992) *Body of Glass*, London: Penguin Books.

Plant, S. (1998) *Zeros + Ones: Digital Women and the New Technoculture*, London: Fourth Estate.

Plato (1987) *The Republic*, Harmondsworth, Middlesex: Penguin (trans. Lee, D., 2nd ed.).

Poovey, M. (1984) *The Proper Lady and the Woman Writer*, Chicago, USA: University of Chicago Press.

Radicalesbians (1970) *The Woman-Identified Woman*, from http://scriptorium.lib.duke.edu/wlm/womid/ (accessed 14th October 2006).

Raphael Reed, L. (1999) 'Troubling Boys and Disturbing Discourses on Masculinity and Schooling: A Feminist Exploration of Current Debates and Interventions Concerning Boys in School' in *Gender and Education*, 11(1) 93-110.

Redstockings. (1969) 'Redstockings Manifesto' in Rosak, B. and Rosak, T. (Eds.) *Masculine/Feminine: Reading in Sexual Mythology and the Liberation of Women*, New York: Harper Colophon Books, 272-274.

Rees, C. (1996) *Utopian Imagination and Eighteenth-Century Fiction*, Harlow, Essex: Longman.

Rich, A. (1977) *Of Woman Born: Motherhood as Experience and Institution*, London: Virago.

Rich, A. (1987a) 'What Does a Woman Need to Know?' in Rich, A. *Blood, Bread and Poetry Selected Prose 1979-1985*, London: Virago Press, 1-10.

Rich, A. (1987b) 'The Soul of A Women's College' in Rich, A. *Blood, Bread and Poetry Selected Prose 1979-1985*, London: Virago Press, 188-197.

Richardson, A. (2002) 'Mary Wollstonecraft on Education' in C. Johnson (Ed.) *The Cambridge Companion to Mary Wollstonecraft*, Cambridge: Cambridge University Press, 24-41.

Riddell, S. and Tett, L. (2006) (Eds.) *Gender and Teaching: Where Have All the Men Gone?*, Edinburgh: Dunedin Academic Press.

Roiphe, K. (1994) *The Morning After: Sex, Fear and Feminism*, London: Hamish Hamilton.

Rosinsky, N. M. (1984) *Feminist Futures: Contemporary Women's Speculative Fiction*, Ann Arbor, Michigan: UMI Research Press.

Rousseau, J. J. (1993) *Emile*, London: Dent.

Rowbotham, S. (1974) *Hidden From History*, London: Pluto Press.

Ruddick, S. (1990) *Maternal Thinking: Towards a Politics of Peace*, London: The Women's Press.

Ruis, M. B. (1999) 'Crossing Border: from Crystal Slippers to Tennis Shoes' in Harcourt, W. *Women @ Internet: Creating New Cultures in Cyberspace*, London: Zed Books, 23-30.

Russ, J. (1985) *The Female Man*, London: The Women's Press.

Russo, M. (1986) 'Female Grotesques: Carnival and Theory' in De Lauretis, T. (Ed.) *Feminist Studies/Cultural Studies*, Bloomington, Indiana: Indiana University Press, 213-229.

Rutter, M. (1981) *Maternal Deprivation: Reassessed*, Harmondsworth, Middlesex: Penguin Books.

Ryan, A. B. (2001) *Feminist Ways of Knowing*, Leicester: NIACE.

Sanders. L. S. (2004) 'Feminist Love a Utopia: Collaboration, Conflict and the Futures of Feminism', in Gillis, S. and Howie, G. (Eds.) *Third Wave Feminism: A Critical Exploration*, Houndsmill Basingstoke, Hampshire: Palgrave, 49-59.

Sandoval, C. (1999) 'New Sciences: Cyborg Feminism and the Methodology of the Oppressed' in Wolmark, J. (Ed.) *Cybersexualities; A Reader on Feminist Theory, Cyborgs and Cyberspace*, Edinburgh: Edinburgh University Press, 247-263.

Sarachild, K. (2000) 'A Program for Feminist Consciousness-Raising' in Crow, B.A. (Ed.) *Radical Feminism: A Documentary Reader*, New York: New York University Press, 273-276.

Sargent, L. T. (1975) 'Utopia – The Problem of Definition' in *Extrapolations*, 16(2), 137-148.

Sargent, L. T. (1994) 'The three faces of utopianism revisited' in *Utopian Studies*, 5(1), 1-37.

Sargisson, L. (1996) *Contemporary Feminist Utopianism*, London: Routledge.

Sargisson, L. (2000) *Utopian Bodies and the Politics of Transgression*, London: Routledge.

Sawyer, W. (2006) 'Robust Hope Against the Odds: Successful Schools in Disadvantaged Communities', A Paper presented at the European Conference for Educational Research (ECER), Geneva 13th-15th September 2006.

Schnorrenberg, B. B. (1982) 'A Paradise Like Eve's, Three Eighteenth Century Female Utopias' in *Women's Studies*, 9, 263-73.

Scott, M. (1994) *Trouble and Her Friends*, New York: Torr Books.

Scott, S. (1986) *Millenium Hall*, London: Virago (1st Published in 1762).

Segal, L. (1999) *Why Feminism? Gender, Psychology, Politics*, Cambridge: Polity Press.

Shaw, R. (2003) 'Our Bodies, Ourselves, Technology and Questions of Ethics: Cyberfeminism and the Lived Body' in *Australian Feminist Studies* 18(4), 45-55.

Showalter, E. (1986) 'Feminist Criticism in the Wilderness' in Showalter, E. (Ed.) *The New Feminist Criticism: Essays on Women, Literature and Theory*, London: Virago Press.

Skinner, B. F. (1976) *Walden Two*, London & New York: Macmillan.

Sommers, C. H. (1994) *Who Stole Feminism: How Women Betrayed Women*, New York: Simon and Schuster.

Sommers, C. H. (2000) *The War Against Boys: How Misguided Feminism Is Harming Our Young Men*, New York: Simon and Schuster.

Sommers, C. H. (2001) 'The War Against Boys: How Misguided Feminism is Harming Our Young Men' in *American Experiment Quarterly*, Spring 26-36, from www.americanexperiment.org/uploaded/files/aeqv4n1sommers.pdf

Spender, D. (1995) *Nattering on the Net: Women, Power and Cyberspace*, Melbourne, Australia: Spinifex.

Spender, J. (1986) 'Introduction' in Scott, S. *Millenium Hall*. London: Virago.

Spivak, G. C. (1988) 'Subaltern Studies: Deconstructing Histography' in Spivak, G. C., *In Other Worlds: Essays in Cultural Politics*, 197-221.

Springborg, P. (1997) ''Introduction to a Serious Proposal I and 11' in Astell, M. *A Serious Proposal Parts 1 and II*, London: Pickering and Chatto.

Stafford, W. (2002) *English Feminists and their Opponents in the 1790s: Unsex'd and Proper Females*, Manchester: Manchester University Press.

Staicar, T. (1982) *The Feminine Eye: Science Fiction and the Women Who Write It*, New York: Ungar.

Stone, A. R (1999) 'Will the Real Body Stand Up? Boundary Stories about Virtual Culture' in Wolmark, J. (Ed.) *Cybersexualities; A Reader on Feminist Theory, Cyborgs and Cyberspace*, Edinburgh: Edinburgh University Press, 69-98.

Sunden, J. (2001) 'What Happened to Difference in Cyberspace? The (Re)turn of the She-Cyborg' in *Feminist Media Studies* 1(12) 215-232.

Suvin, D. (1979) *Metamorphoses of Science Fiction: On the Politics and History of a Literary Genre*, New Haven: Yale University Press.

Symington, A. and Sprenger, E. (2004) 'The Future of Women's Rights', Kerr, J., Sprenger, E. and Symington, A. (2004) (Eds.) *The Future of Women's Rights*, London/New York: Zed Books, 1-13.

Taylor, B. (1985) *Eve and the New Jerusalem Socialism and Feminism in the 19th Century*, London: Virago.

Third Wave Foundation (2006) *Third Wave Foundation*, from http://www.thirdwavefoundation.org/ (accessed 12th November 2006)

Tinklin, T. (2003) 'Gender Differences and High Attainment', in *British Educational Research Journal* 29 (3), 307-324.

Tizard, B. and Hughes, M. (1984) *Young Children Learning: Thinking and Talking at Home*, London: Fontana.

Todd, J. (1989) *The Sign of Angellica: Women, Writing and Fiction 1660-1800*, New York: Columbia University Press.

Todd, J. (1996) 'Introduction' in Todd, J. (Ed.) *Female Education in the Age of Enlightenment*, Vol. 1, London: William Pickering, vii-xiii.

Todd, J. (2004) *Rebel Daughters*, London: Penguin.

Tuana, N. (1993) *The Less Noble Sex Scientific, Religious and Philosophical Conceptions of Woman's Nature*, Bloomington, Indiana: Indiana University Press.

UNICEF (2005) *Gender Achievements and Prospects in Education: The GAP Report Part 1*, New York: UNICEF, from http://ungei.org/gap/pdfs/unicef_gap_low_res.pdf (accessed 11th November 2006)

United Nations Children's Fund (1990) *Goals for Children and Development in the 1990s*, New York: UNICEF.

United Nations Educational, Scientific and Cultural Organization (2006) *Strong Foundations: Early Childhood Care and Education: Education for All Global Monitoring Report*, Paris: UNESCO.

VNS Matrix (1991) *Cyberfeminist Manifesto for the 21st Century* from http://www.sterneck.net/cybertribe/cyber/vns-matrix/index.php (accessed 11th November 2006).

Vonarburg, E. (1992) *In Mothers' Land*, USA: Bantam (Originally in French, Maerlande trans. Brierley, J.).

Walkerdine, V. and Lucey, H. (1986) *Democracy in the Kitchen*, London: Virago Press.

Walters, N. (1999) *The New Feminism*, London: Virago.

Weiler, K. (1991) 'Friere and a Feminist Pedagogy of Difference' in *Harvard Educational Review* 61, 449-474.

Whelehan, I. (2000) *Overloaded: Popular Culture and the Future of Feminism*, London: The Women's Press.

Whyte, J., Deem, R., Kant, L. and Cruickshank, M. (Eds.) (1975) *Girl Friendly Schooling*, London: Methuen.

Wilding, F. (1997) *Where is Feminism in Cyberfeminism* from http://www.andrew.cmu.edu/user/fwild/faithwilding/wherefem.html (accessed 8th November 2006).

Wilding, F. and the Arts Ensemble (1997) *Notes on the Political Condition of Cyberfeminism*, from http://www.obn.org/cfundef/condition.html (accessed 8th November 2006).

Williams, R. (1980) 'Utopia and Science Fiction' in Williams, R. *Problems in Materialism and Culture*. London: Verso Books, 196-212.

Wittig, M. (1992a) 'The Category of Sex' in Wittig, M. *The Straight Mind and Other Essays*, Hemel Hempstead, Hert.: Harvester Wheatsheaf Press, 1-9.

Wittig, M. (1992b) 'One Is Not Born A Woman', in Wittig, M. *The Straight Mind and Other Essays*, Hemel Hempstead, Hert.: Harvester Wheatsheaf Press, 9-20.

Wolf, N. (1991) *The Beauty Myth: How Images of Beauty Are Used against Women*, London: Vintage.

Wollstonecraft, M. (1994) *Thoughts on the Education of Daughters*, Oxford and New York: Woodstock Books (1st Published 1787).

Wollstonecraft, M. (1790) 'Review of Letters on Education: With Observations on Religious and Metaphysical Subjects in Analytical Review Volume VIII', in Butler M. and Todd. J. (1989) *The Works of Mary Wollstonecraft*, Vol. 7 309-322.

Wollstonecraft, M. (1988) 'A Vindication of the Rights of Women', in Poston, C. (Ed.) (1988) *A Vindication of the Rights of Woman*, London: Norton 1-194, 2nd ed.

Wolmark, J. (1993) *Aliens and Others: Science Fiction, Feminism and Postmodernism*, Hemel Hempstead: Harvester Wheatsheaf.

Wolmark, J. (Ed.) *Cybersexualities; A Reader on Feminist Theory, Cyborgs and Cyberspace*, Edinburgh: Edinburgh University Press.
Women's Collective (N.D.) *Consciousness-Raising*, from: http://Cwluherstory.Com/Cwluarchive/Crgguidelines.html (accessed 22nd December 2006)

INDEX

Printed in the United Kingdom
by Lightning Source UK Ltd.
124706UK00002B/337/A

9 789087 900571